LEADING THE WAY

LEADING THE WAY

INSPIRING WORDS FOR WOMEN

ON HOW TO LIVE AND LEAD WITH COURAGE,
CONFIDENCE, AND AUTHENTICITY

FROM INTERVIEWS BY
MARIANNE SCHNALL

EDITED BY
ANGELA JOSHI

TILLER PRESS

New York London Toronto Sydney New Delhi

TILLER PRESS

An Imprint of Simon & Schuster, Inc.
1230 Avenue of the Americas
New York, NY 10020

First Tiller Press trade paperback edition September 2019

TILLER PRESS and colophon are trademarks of Simon & Schuster, Inc.

For information about special discounts for bulk purchases, please contact Simon & Schuster Special Sales at 1-866-506-1949 or business@simonandschuster.com.

The Simon & Schuster Speakers Bureau can bring authors to your live event. For more information or to book an event, contact the Simon & Schuster Speakers Bureau at 1-866-248-3049 or visit our website at www.simonspeakers.com.

Interior design by Jaime Putorti
Jacket design by Patrick Sullivan

Manufactured in the United States of America

10 9 8 7 6 5 4 3 2 1

Library of Congress Cataloging-in-Publication Data is available.

ISBN 978-1-9821-3091-6
ISBN 978-1-9821-3092-3 (ebook)

To my amazing daughters, Lotus and Jazmin, who have been my greatest blessings, inspirations, and teachers, and to all the other magnificent women and girls in the world who are leading the way.

CONTENTS

INTRODUCTION

Throughout my thirty-year career as a journalist, I've interviewed some of today's most influential women and men—celebrities, CEOs, politicians, filmmakers, authors, activists, and more—and I've heard them all express one resounding message: the world needs more women leaders.

Women make up more than half of the population of this country, yet we are still vastly underrepresented in leadership across every sector of society, where solutions to problems are being created and important decisions are being made. Without women's voices and visions, as actress Natalie Portman put it to me, "We're missing out on fifty percent of our potential great people." And as activist and author Robin Morgan aptly pointed out, "We need all hands on deck."

Today we are on the verge of a tipping point. Simultaneous to all of the concerning problems we face in this country and around the world, a potent force has been unleashed and is growing: the power and influence of women. From the Women's March and the #MeToo movement to the historic numbers of women running for and winning seats in elected office and an unprecedented number of women running for president in 2020, women everywhere are rising up and speaking out. There is a growing awareness and concern for the glaring lack of equity between the sexes, especially given the benefits of having gender diversity (and diversity of all types) across all industries, and this has resulted in a loud and urgent demand for change.

Yet progress for advancing women's leadership has been exceedingly slow across the board—in the corporate world, politics, media, finance, and other industries—and there remains a variety of structural, cultural, and psychological obstacles and challenges that stand in the way of achieving this progress. That is why I decided to publish *Leading the Way*: to celebrate and amplify all that women bring to leadership, to offer solutions to counteract some of the negative influences that inhibit women's leadership, and to provide inspiration, guidance, and encouragement to anyone who wants to advocate for change and help us get closer to parity.

As much as the larger objective of this book is to help more women become leaders across industries and in our government, *Leading the Way* also advocates for women to step into leadership in their own lives: to be their authentic selves; follow their true calling; achieve their full potential; be effective advocates for themselves, others, and the causes they care about; and live lives that are aligned not only with who they truly are but also with what brings them fulfillment, connection, well-being, and joy.

I have been so fortunate that my personal leadership journey has been intertwined with and shaped by the stories and insights I have heard firsthand from the extraordinary changemakers I have interviewed or interacted with during my career. I have soaked up and benefited from so much wisdom, energy, inspiration, and sisterhood along the way.

Whether it was through interviewing luminaries and trailblazers like Maya Angelou, Oprah Winfrey, Madeleine Albright, Nancy Pelosi, and Anita Hill; hearing gentle words of guidance whispered into my ear by Gloria Steinem; or witnessing Eve Ensler sit at my dining room table and birth the idea for her global activist movement, V-Day, which has gone on to raise more than $100 million to help end violence against women and girls worldwide, I feel so blessed to have seen firsthand the incredible change that is possible when women overcome their obstacles, dig deep into their truest selves, and pursue their dreams.

Having personally experienced how powerful and influential the words of these leaders can be, I felt compelled to share some of their quotes and wisdom in this book to encourage women to know their power, use their voices, and be agents of change—in their personal lives, their communities, and the larger world. In these pages, you'll find insights from a wide range of remarkable figures I've interviewed over the years, on topics including knowing your worth and finding a work-life balance, to modeling new paradigms of leadership and power, to uplifting marginalized voices, and so much more.

My hope is that the messages in this book will give you more confidence and courage to share your unique abilities and ideas, remind you that your voice matters, and inspire you to step up as a leader in whatever ways feel right to you. There are so many ways we as women can be leaders and contribute to the world, but it all starts with knowing and valuing who we are and what it is we uniquely bring to the table. When we support each other and work together, we are a hugely powerful, transformative force.

As Senator Kirsten Gillibrand told me in one of our interviews, which, unbeknownst to me at the time, foreshadowed the title for this book: "We need women *leading the way*. I really think that until women are able to achieve their potential, America will not achieve hers."

Always remember that you are a magnificent force for change and that you have what it takes to help lead the way to a better, more equal, and just world.

LEADING
THE WAY

1

CREATE NEW PARADIGMS OF LEADERSHIP AND POWER

*Get over the feeling that the two words don't go together—
women and power. The fact is, if we don't put the two
together and don't understand how power changes
complexion in the hands of women, then we're not going
to make it. We have to own our personal power.*
—Jane Fonda

Throughout my career interviewing successful women leaders, one important point that consistently comes up is the notion that if women are going to advance into more positions of power, we shouldn't mimic the ways power and leadership have been modeled for us throughout history so far (mostly by men). Instead, we should model new paradigms of power and bring our authentic voices and full selves to our leadership. Oftentimes, the leadership qualities that are most celebrated and promoted in our culture are mainly what are characterized as the "masculine" ones: being tough, strong, and authoritative—and thinking of power in hierarchical ways. But we need to shift this perception so that good leadership also includes women's unique sets of experiences and perspectives, as well as qualities that are generally deemed "feminine," such as compassion, empathy, or having a collaborative spirit.

Women—and men, since leadership stereotypes can constrict them, too—should be able to embrace these feminine attributes of leadership so that we can begin to disrupt those gender stereotypes and bring a full range of human qualities to leadership. We also need to reframe the purpose of power as not simply having power for one's own benefit, but instead as a means to use our influence to guide, empower, and uplift those who don't have power: to give power *to* rather than have power *over*.

After all, why have more women in leadership if we are not going to bring all we have to offer to the table? To inspire you to start leading in your own way and on your own terms, I've included insights in this chapter from several successful women leaders who are all examples and advocates of power and leadership done differently.

A new power paradigm emerges when a different gender holds it, has it, and then uses it differently. I mean, if women get power only to be just like the guys who had it before them, then that's not progress.

—PAT MITCHELL

For the first time in a long time, women are understanding that we do have power and we need to learn to exercise it.

—MAXINE WATERS

Women view power differently. It's not power *over*; it's power *with*. It's about empowering others. Now, there are some women who view power the way men do, but generally speaking, women do it differently. It's not hierarchical; it's circular.

—JANE FONDA

Women in leadership suffer from stereotyping, and when people expect a stereotype and are reminded of a stereotype, that actually makes the stereotype stronger. It's called stereotype threat, and it's why when women check off "Miss" or girls check off "Female" before taking a math test, the research shows they actually do worse. What has happened is that there aren't women in leadership roles. Therefore, people don't expect there to be women in leadership roles. Therefore, there aren't women in leadership roles.

It's the classic chicken-and-egg problem. We need more women leaders to show more women they can lead, and we need to show more women they can lead to get more women leaders. I think the first thing we need to do is decide that the status quo is not okay.

The word "female," when inserted in front of something, is always with a note of surprise. Female COO, female pilot, female surgeon—as if ["female"] implies surprise, which it does. I am a female leader. One day there won't be "female" leaders. There will just be leaders.

—SHERYL SANDBERG

I think women, like men, should pursue their talents and interests. I believe that it is only a matter of time before the structural barriers to women or minorities are effectively dismantled. I look forward to the day when I am thought of as the 102nd Supreme Court Justice rather than the first female Supreme Court Justice.

—SANDRA DAY O'CONNOR

The leadership qualities that are needed to really propel things forward are feminine, and both men and women need to draw on these attributes because the times are calling for it. You know, I've always had a thing for "C" words. Create. Connect. Collaborate. Communicate. Change. Compassion. Community. These are the words I've leaned on in my own experience as a leader, and when I really look at these words, I see how they are all about feminine leadership.

I believe we have been living in a very masculine world; a world of singularity where we are not looking at things holistically, where we don't take in the totality of a woman. It's been a boys' club, and leadership and the way we think about it has been impacted by this. In order for things to change, we have to shift the perspective from being "either/or" to "and." It's not about women replacing men—it's about the embrace. We need masculine and feminine energies for us to move the needle forward. I feel that there is a dynamic shift that is happening and that a balance needs to be restored.

—DONNA KARAN

I think it takes a while for women to realize what their power is, because we haven't been part of this for very long. But what I have seen is that when women know their power, they really do know how to use it, not for their personal gain, but for the good of the country. There's a big difference there between how women operate versus how men operate. Women know how to wield their power, and from what I see, it's almost always for the greater good.

—BARBARA LEE

We must encourage other women to step up to positions of leadership—women who understand the glass ceiling that still exists for us in the workplace and in every aspect of our lives and who are committed to helping us shatter that ceiling once and for all. . . . Because what we really need are more women opening doors in every aspect of our society—more women practicing law, more women researching cures for cancer, more women in information technology, and more women in public office.

—DEBBIE WASSERMAN SCHULTZ

I think it's embedded in the psychology of women, men, girls, boys, nations, organizations, and schools that what it takes to lead is anathema to what we have told ourselves is appropriate and charming for a woman. It's so deep in our psyche. It's deeper than we know. No matter how liberated we are as individual women and how much work we've put into convincing ourselves of our inherent equality with men, we still don't even believe it ourselves. And how could we? It's embedded in every part of our culture. There's religion; there's art, the greatest authors, the greatest playwrights; there's the hero's journey. Every single mythology and area of human expertise is still, either consciously or unconsciously, pervaded by the idea that it is beautiful for a man to exert his ego, his will, and his leadership, and it is beautiful and charming for a woman to defer, to support, to nurture, and not to push her way and her will.

What would happen if women could lead from their core basic values? Not just put women into a structure that is up-down power like, "I have power over you," but what if women could actually influence the way power is wielded in the world from a core feminine place?

Years ago, I began thinking about what happens when you put the words "women" and "power" together. From the beginning of recorded history, there's been an unspoken law that it's unladylike to put those words together. I wanted to turn that on its head and explore the whole issue. What is a powerful woman? As women assume more power, can we transform the way it is used? Can we help the world become more conscious about the uses and abuses of power?

We believe women have the potential to change the way power is used in the world for everybody. We're not interested in women taking over the old power paradigm. We think everyone will benefit when women not only join men at the table but also help men turn the tables over and create something new. When the rules of power were made—way back in the early stages of human society-building—women weren't part of the conversation. They weren't consulted on questions like, "How do we share resources? How do we deal with conflict? What should we prioritize? What's important for a society?"

As women take on more and more powerful leadership positions—in the home, at work, in religion, and government—when enough of us get there, we might actually change what it means to be powerful and to lead. It might look more inclusive. It might look like a more care-based society. This has never been tested, because there have never been enough women in power and enough women empowered with their own voice to even test it. Our loftiest goal is to ask these questions of women leaders: "Can you show, in your leadership, a different way of dealing with conflict—a more constructive way of sharing power? Do you have better reasons for wanting to lead than just to satisfy your own ego? Are you interested in leadership as a way of transforming our society?"

I don't know exactly what it will look like when there's full inclusivity of women, but I have to assume that any group who has been left out for that long has something really important to add to the whole picture to balance things out. A critical mass of women of all different points of view is going to make a difference.

—ELIZABETH LESSER

I think the world is realizing that [empowering and educating girls and women] is incredibly important and that we need to do more and more to support women, because in many parts of the developing world their power is often very limited. And yet in so many cases, the power they have to make decisions is the key to their families' future. I think people need to remember that empowering women to determine their future should not be controversial, no matter where you are.

—MELINDA GATES

Power is something you have to take and use. It's just not given to you. The only thing you get is what you fight for and nothing more. We've just got to be willing to make more people uncomfortable and push for the power that we deserve.

—CECILE RICHARDS

It's hitting in on a number of fronts. It's getting more women in the pipeline in every area toward power. That's in the pipeline toward power in the corporate world and changing the ethics there. It's toward getting women more power in politics, in the entertainment industry, you name it.

—ROBIN MORGAN

Women have to be taught that ambition is ladylike and that having ambition is important for their families. What women have to realize is that power is the *ultimate* security. Power brings about a much broader type of security for their children and for their grandchildren. So get comfortable around the notion of participating fully in the process *and* that ambition is something that should be admired in a woman.

I remember when I was very young and a state representative, and they wrote a feature about me for the Kansas City paper titled "Blonde Ambition," and I remember cringing when I saw the headline. And then I caught myself and thought, *Well, now why are you so worried that they're saying you are ambitious?* I was naturally uncomfortable that somebody had called me out on being ambitious. So I think our young ladies, our young women, my daughters, their daughters, all need to understand that ambition is an important form of getting security for you and your family and for the values that you are committed to.

—CLAIRE McCASKILL

When you talk about "girl power," even that's sort of a belittling thing; they won't call it "women's power" because that is somehow too dangerous. Girl power, that's okay—that's somehow defanged and acceptable, whereas women's power is terrifying and emasculating. So there's even a problem in language, there's a problem in the media, there's a problem in society. There are just so many things challenging girls and women in their search for power and strength that we need to do all we can to help that along.

—MARGARET CHO

There's an imbalance and you can really feel it in the way everything is going, I think. Sometimes I feel like it's a bit of a fallacy to try and say, "Men are violent and women are nonviolent," because I don't think that's necessarily true. But I do think there is a sort of natural balance in nature between men and women, and that it's being thrown off-balance by the social and economic inequities between men and women.

—NATALIE PORTMAN

Sometimes we romanticize the role that the women can play, because in many countries of the world, women are still not in charge. They are still not playing a very important role in decision-making. But sometimes when women do find themselves in those positions, we really don't see that much difference. And I have always felt that perhaps women have sometimes almost embraced the same values as men, and the same character as men, because they are in the men's world, and they are trying to fit into a system that men have created. And maybe, in truth, when there is a critical mass of women who play that role in governments, such as what we have in Rwanda, then we will see whether women can really manage power in a way that is less destructive than the way that men have used power.

—WANGARI MAATHAI

Power is the ability to empower yourself and others. We are moving into a partnership society, and the only power that works is partnership power. The new business model is: If I do well, I'll teach you how to do well, and we'll all rise together. The old model is: I will be the president of the bank or on the board of the bank and we will have these huge bonuses and the tellers will get just above minimum wage. The new model is a partnership model, and if you look at the compensation plan of a network marketing company, you will see that you can't possibly do well unless you're helping others succeed, too, and everyone has the same opportunity going in. The playing field is absolutely level.

—DR. CHRISTIANE NORTHRUP

I'm less interested now in "power" than I am in freedom. I have been asking deep questions about the meaning of power, the nature of power. One of the things we're working on with the One Billion Rising campaign is to let everybody own it and have it and use it the way they need to use it. That's the power I'm interested in—a kind of energetic power that gets to be shared and gets to circulate, where everybody gets to feed off it, like wind.

—EVE ENSLER

To be a leader for today's world, you have to engage with people who are different from you, and you have to be able to listen. You have to pay attention. Everybody's voice needs to be listened to—heard with respect and heard on its own terms. So it really boils down to somebody who's capable of paying attention, who's capable of listening, who's engaged in a search for mutual understanding, who understands cooperation, who has the capacity not only to think clearly but to respond to the feelings of their own and other people. It's very, very basic human qualities, and all the research in the human sciences is saying as humans, this is who we are. We are responsive, relational beings. Our nervous systems are wired to connect thought with emotion. We all have a voice. We want to be heard. We want to live in relationship.

A leader for today's world has to basically be someone in whom those human capacities are well developed.

—CAROL GILLIGAN

When women think of power, we shouldn't think of it only for ourselves. We should be thinking about what we're going to do with power once we have it. Women should be standing up powerfully and passionately for the care and protection of children, as well as the care and protection of the earth itself.

Women's voices should be front and center in protecting both our young and our habitat. That's the way it is in any species that survives.

—MARIANNE WILLIAMSON

One of the reasons why I want women to run things is because when we run things, when we actually have power, we run things differently. We not only don't abuse power, we also share it. And we create the environment for others to lead, for there to be policies that really challenge the idea that everything is a zero-sum game.

If you look at the Women's March as an example, there were signs about every issue under the sun. Everything from health care to education to mass incarceration to immigration, and there was room for all of it. We didn't have to choose, we didn't have to prioritize, and it actually felt right. And so when women run things, we actually know how to hold the complexity of American life in the twenty-first century and actually move us all toward solutions together. We need leaders who can unify the country, not tear us apart. We need leaders who can actually open more space for voices to be heard. We need leaders who can democratize the story of who we are as a country, as opposed to take us back in history. Take us forward—women can do that.

—AI-JEN POO

Q&A WITH PAT MITCHELL ON WOMEN USING POWER IN THEIR OWN WAY

The most important thing as a woman leader . . . is that if you have a position of leadership and power and you don't use it in a different way, then you're wasting it.
—Pat Mitchell

Pat Mitchell is a media executive and lifelong advocate for women and girls. At every step of her career, Mitchell has broken new ground for women by leveraging the power of media as a journalist and as an Emmy Award–winning and Oscar-nominated producer to tell women's stories and increase the representation of women onscreen and off. She became the president of CNN Productions, and the first woman president and CEO of PBS and the Paley Center for Media. Today, her commitment to connect and strengthen a global community of women leaders continues as a conference curator, advisor, and mentor.

In partnership with TED, Mitchell launched TEDWomen in 2010 and is its editorial director, curator, and host. Mitchell is active with many nonprofit organizations, serving as the chair of the boards for the Sundance Institute and the Women's Media Center, and she is a founding member of the V-Day movement. She is the author of Becoming a Dangerous Woman: Embracing Risk to Change the World.

MARIANNE SCHNALL: What are some of your thoughts on how women view and use power?

PAT MITCHELL: Power in our lifetimes has been defined by the dominant gender who has it. And a lot of the way they have defined power is not something we as women are comfortable with, nor would we want to carry out power in that way. So we move away from the current definitions and current manifestations of power. We are talking about redefining power, putting a woman's perspective on it.

A shift in the power paradigm in this country is absolutely essential. We know that very few people in history ever give up power voluntarily. Why is that? And yet women give it away all the time because it is a way in which women approach power: sharing it. Well, of course that's a great way to look at power, but how do we get that to be the power paradigm, as it were, the prevailing power? By getting power and using it that way, using it in a way that shares it, that redefines it, that gives it other adjectives than the ones we attach to it now.

MS: Why does gender parity matter?

PM: Not only is gender equality or gender parity a right that belongs to all women, but gender equality makes for a better world. It creates a more inclusive marketplace, which, by the way, is more successful and delivers a better bottom line. It brings prosperity, peace, and security to families and communities. You look around the world and you see where women have greater equality and have access on an equal basis to opportunity, and you're going

to see a society that is more prosperous, more peaceful, more sustainable. And all of that comes from a woman's perspective on
how she can lead.

MS: **You have broken so many barriers, being the first
woman president and CEO of PBS, and so many different
accomplishments—you really are a trailblazer. What insights
can you offer about being a woman leader?**

PM: In my opinion, the most important thing as a woman leader—
and I learned this early through a whole bunch of great women
who were in my life, and men, I have to say—is that if you have a
position of leadership and power and you don't use it in a different way, then you're wasting it. So when people used to say to me
when I was the first woman president of PBS, "Does that mean
that as a woman you're going to be a different kind of president?"
And I would say, "Well, I hope so!"

I decided a long, long time ago, when I was one of the first
women in television, that while in the beginning I went along with
avoiding at all costs anything that brought attention to the fact
that I was a woman, very quickly I learned that didn't feel good to
me, and also I thought it was really letting myself down.

So as a woman leader, you can't make every decision from that
point of view, but my experience is as a mother, as a grandmother,
a wife, a sister, a daughter—all those things—I tried to keep them
in mind, because I know they're a part of me. So if I'm not bringing
them to the table as the CEO or the executive producer or the host
or whatever it may be, then I'm denying part of who I am and that
means I'm not going to be as good as I could be.

MS: What characteristics do you think women bring to leadership?

PM: Women bring to leadership an attitude, a different set of attributes, different visions, different life paths, and all of that can make for transformative change leaders. . . . There's been so much debate about whether women do make different kinds of leaders. I believe we do. Because I believe that women are changing the nature of power, rather than power changing the nature of women. We are bringing to power natural, feminine attributes that come to us from our own life experiences as mothers and sisters and daughters and wives. If we bring all this to bear into our leadership positions, then we will be different kinds of leaders.

Women have a lot of the attributes that make great leaders: empathy, vision, resilience, courage, the ability to create community, to mobilize support, to listen, and to act. Those are the qualities that we need for the kinds of changes necessary. So I believe we need women in leadership positions and we need those women to speak, and lead, in a woman's voice.

MS: Why do you think there is still a hurdle to women becoming elected leaders on the national stage? What must we do to combat that narrative as a culture that women don't belong in leadership?

PM: There are still so many hurdles to women achieving leadership positions, particularly in government. Some of them began in the way in which we actually cover and present women as candidates, and for that we have to look to the media who have always held women candidates to different standards, covered their campaigns differently, and that has to change. Women have less access to money—fundraising is always a bigger challenge for women candidates than it is traditionally for men. That has to change. And in some societies, of course, women are blocked from even entering the public sphere. But in our country we're in the public sphere, and in that sphere we can have a greater voice, I believe, if we do one thing: support each other.

MS: What are your thoughts on how women in leadership can bring up other women with them?

PM: Men are very good at building networks, but they don't do it out of maleness. They do it to make sure the power paradigm continues. They build the networks with the people that they want to keep in power and not give up the power. Women build networks of friendship and support. We have to be just as conscious. If you're sitting in a powerful position, it is an absolute number one responsibility in my opinion to look around and see, is there some woman who is in that position who needs to have that extra pull up? One of my favorite lines was always, "Every step of the ladder you take up, look at who's on the step behind and give her a helping hand." That should not be unique to men or women, but men already do that. They may not do it for the same motivations, but they're doing it. So our motivations ought to be: We still need to raise women up, and every position we have is an opportunity to do that.

MS: What is one message you would like to share to inspire people to advocate for more women in leadership and to push for gender equity?

PM: It's time for women. Everything points to it. We need new leadership, we need new vision, we need new directions! And women are standing ready and prepared to do that—to lead their communities and their countries. So what it's going to take, and what we need more than anything else, is women who are courageous, willing to take the risk, and have the vision and the commitment to step forward and say, "I'm ready to serve." And then for the rest of us to be there to support them in whatever it is they decide to do to bring about greater gender equity.

2

WHAT WOMEN BRING

It isn't that women coming in are better than men; they're different from men. And I always say the beauty is in the mix. To have diversity of opinion in the debate strengthens the outcome and you get a better result.

—Nancy Pelosi

Why is it essential to have more women leaders? One of the points I think is important to make is that it isn't just about fairness and equality. It's also about having a more representative society and better representation within all of our institutions. While I try to steer away from making broad generalizations, a lot of people I've interviewed have mentioned that women, specifically, have a range of valuable traits suited for leadership, like being good listeners and communicators, consensus builders, and natural collaborators.

As many of the female elected officials I've interviewed have observed, women have a tendency to reach out across the aisle to find common ground—a worthy attribute we certainly need in the hyper-divided and partisan world we live in today. We have seen numerous examples of this in practice, such as the bipartisan effort of female senators brokering an end to a government shut-down in 2013, and many more in politics, the corporate world, and beyond.

Having more women in leadership and at decision-making tables also brings greater diversity, which has been proven in all sectors to benefit innovation, productivity, and the bottom line. Also, as women, we always bring our unique set of experiences to our work. So, for example, when discussing political issues that impact us—whether it has to do with women's health, violence against women, reproductive freedom, or addressing sexual harassment—women need to be able to convey our absolutely essential perspectives. We've all seen the all-male panels in Washington, DC, discussing topics such as sexual assault in the military or women's health. Women *must* be seated at those tables to share our realities and experiences and help come up with effective solutions.

As I always like to say, working to have more women in leadership isn't a "women's" issue, it's a *human* issue. We all benefit from the contributions women bring.

The world is looking at women now and saying, "This is your moment," in everything from studies by Ernst & Young and McKinsey and many others that tell us businesses that have more women in top leadership positions make more money, to a *constant* flow of leadership-oriented books, articles, and speeches that say the characteristics that women bring to the workplace are exactly the kind of leadership we need today—in politics, in business, in any sphere of life.

The attention to relationships. The tendency to want to collaborate. The notion that power doesn't have to be about power *over* someone, but rather it's the power *to.* It's the power of possibility. It's the power of making good things happen. Making the world better for my family, my kids, my community, my world. That's how women can really make a difference.

If we shift how we're thinking about power from that old-fashioned, patriarchal, hierarchical, traditional power *over* to the expansive, innovative, infinite power *to,* it just changes everything. And it allows women who have been resisting taking powerful positions to take those positions.

—GLORIA FELDT

I can say this without any doubt, I have no hesitation: women bring a consensus-building attitude that is not always present at the table. When I first became Speaker, people would come to me and say, "Do you know how different this meeting would have been if a man had been running it?" We build consensus; we don't dictate policy.

Secondly, I really do believe that women have an intuitive sense, which is very important in leadership. If you have a vision and you have knowledge and you have a plan, you know what decision you need to make intuitively. And that confidence is contagious. If you act in that decisive a way, people will have confidence in you, and they'll follow your lead.

—NANCY PELOSI

I think there *is* reason to think that there are some substantive differences in how women govern, both stylistically and in terms of the policy output. And that's just the empirical work of women in politics—scholars who show us that, in fact, when you have more women in a state legislature, for example, you're more likely to have real bipartisan bills passed, that women tend to introduce more legislation on issues of the environment and education than their male colleagues. So there do, in fact, seem to be substantive reasons for having women.

—MELISSA HARRIS-PERRY

It's probable that walking around female for twenty years or fifty years in this culture has given someone a set of experiences that men don't necessarily have—in the same way that walking around as a black person or a Hispanic person or a gay person gives people a different set of experiences than a white, heterosexual person. Experience is everything. Somebody who has experienced something is more expert at it than the experts.

—GLORIA STEINEM

In a legislative body, you need the variety of life experiences. I learned this when I was in the state legislature and when I was in the Senate. In the state legislature, I passed a bill for the fair treatment of rape victims. And when we got the bill to the floor, the men weren't against it, they had just never had the experience of the unfairness of the judicial system for rape victims. And we then passed a law that became the model in America, because every state was lacking in fair treatment.

When I got to the Senate, I teamed up with Barbara Mikulski for the Hutchison/Mikulski bill that was the Homemaker IRA, and it was because of an experience I had: I was single, I started an IRA; I got married and couldn't contribute the same amount to my IRA. They allowed $250 for a spouse, which is, I mean, you might as well not do it. And yet you could put aside $2,500 if you had a job. And I said, "No way is it [fair]—women who work inside the home should have the same retirement opportunities that women who work outside the home have." Nobody was against it—it was just that they never thought of it before. They'd never had the experience. You need the variety of experience to be able to represent the variety of the people.

—KAY BAILEY HUTCHISON

There is a real difference in the way women practice power. If you've come up through cigar-smoking, backroom-deal party politics, for example, like Margaret Thatcher did, you're going to be an imitation guy, which is what Margaret Thatcher was. We're not talking about that. And we're not talking about a token.

We're talking about, for example, in Norway, when Gro Harlem Brundtland was first elected prime minister. She appointed a few women, and her policies were not that markedly different on environment and other things. Being a Scandinavian country, they were already basically pretty damn liberal compared to us, but they weren't that different from what they had been before. Then she lost in an election. Then she came back and she was reelected, and the second time she was elected, she appointed the majority of her cabinet women, and everything suddenly changed. In other words, not tokenism, but critical mass. Policies on everything from employment and childcare and flextime and work hours to environmental policies to you name it—it just changed. It was absolutely enormous. So there's a very real difference.

Now, why that difference is, people can disagree about until the sun goes down. I think it's a combination. I don't think it's either/or. I don't think it's bifurcated. I think it's a both/and. I think it's a combination of biology and socialization. Socialization, we know, raises women to take care of and be caregivers and, if anything, be afraid of power. They're afraid of power the way it's been defined by men: power *over*. When you reposition it as power *to*, they're not afraid of power anymore.

And, biologically, the more that we now begin to get emerging evidence of value-free tests and value-free science, we learn things like the fight-or-flight defense that we thought was characteristic of all humans in a crisis situation—adrenaline fuels fight or flight. Well, everybody experiences it to some degree, but, interestingly enough, where it is most pronounced is in men. What women have in crisis situations, at the same time as the release of adrenaline, is a release of oxytocin, which is the caregiving, bonding, empathetic chemical, which does not release at the same time in men. This was a University of California study that first evinced it and named it the "tend-and-befriend" reaction. So in men you get fight or flight. In women you get tend and befriend. That's a *huge*, humongous difference. And these are science based; these are not crazy feminist fantasies.

So I think there is both a biological reason and, certainly, a socialized reason why women govern differently from men.

—ROBIN MORGAN

Women's lives are very different. We have different life experiences, and our differences are our strength. We will bring knowledge of issues to the fore, we will raise different issues, and we will offer different solutions.

I think a woman's perspective often will complement a male's perspective. In fact, oftentimes we see the problem differently, we see the solution differently, and so by bringing that perspective to the table, you will have a more holistic approach. For example, women are often very good listeners, often good consensus builders, often able to compromise and reach across party lines in Congress, able to forge deals and reach better solutions. So I think by nature we are very good at consensus building, but we also often seek political office for different reasons. Many women come to political life because they want to solve problems or address a certain issue that they care deeply about—less often are they coming to Washington for power or self-aggrandizement.

—KIRSTEN GILLIBRAND

There's been a lot of research into how men and women lead differently—research that tells you women are more collaborative, and I've read a bunch of that. But what I think is more powerful is you come from this outsider perspective, so when you take your seat at the table, you don't necessarily ask all the same questions that other people would. You don't necessarily bring with you all the same people that other people would. You bring a different perspective, a different background.

—SOLEDAD O'BRIEN

It's not just about women rising; it's about men rising, too. I know that sounds counterintuitive, but I think that feminism means supporting men *and* women to create equality that makes our societies better, our relationships better, our opportunities better. Basically, if we can create this kind of full equality and understanding between men and women, what we're going to do is we're going to allow ideas to rise that help us take down poverty and take down human suffering on a new level. So I think of it as being a benefit to society, not just about a benefit to women.

—ANN CURRY

Women will broaden the information that goes into decision-making. I think people tend to connect with and bring into their own circles people who are like them, so by bringing in one person, you are more likely to bring additional women voices into the decision-making process, and that's going to be better for everyone if the perspective is broadened. I think we've got so many complex issues that cannot be resolved by looking at them from one perspective. And ultimately, allowing more women in will help make better decisions if, in fact, those women are powerful and in tune with and connected with other women's voices, and perhaps voices of people who have been left out of the conversation, including people of color.

—ANITA HILL

There is very solid evidence that more diverse groups come up with better decisions, and people who study decision-making have typically found that the group that comes out with the most optimal results is not the group containing the most optimal individuals, but rather the most diverse individuals.

I think that if we don't have gender diversity at the top of American politics and in corporate boards, then we're just going to get weaker decisions, and I think that's what we've been stuck with. . . . Women bring a certain level of different perspective, a different way of thinking, and that is just really valuable for all of us. This is not something that is just going to benefit the women of America; it's something that's going to benefit all of America.

—NICHOLAS KRISTOF

We are a better nation when the people who represent us are true representatives of who we are. If we have people who represent us who don't share our values or don't share our adventures or our backgrounds and they don't understand us—we just don't have those voices crying out for the issues that we care about—then we're a poorer nation for it. Women represent such an important part of our society, whether it's electorally or in economics or in every facet of life. And it doesn't mean that women care about only issues A, B, and C. Of course we're just as good at multitasking as the men are; we are as interested in defense as we are in daycare issues. So it's not just the issues that we're involved with, but it's a different way of looking at the world.

Not all women, of course, are the same, but it's an important voice that is missing—just as we don't have enough Hispanics and we don't have enough blacks represented in Fortune 500 companies. When you look at the boards of directors in those companies, you're just aghast. We look like we're a progressive organization in Congress when you compare it to the big companies and how much they lack diversity.

—ILEANA ROS-LEHTINEN

I used to think [representation of women] was important because it was unfair. And now I understand it's important because it fundamentally creates a different environment, which is not to say that every woman is different from every man or that all men and women are totally different, but to say that when women are an incredible mass in the organizations, the organizations tend to function differently—because women bring in critical mass, a really important, different way of understanding things. They have conversations longer, which might be annoying to people, but when they agree, they really agree. They are better on consensus, they manufacture relationships—everywhere they go they turn it into a relationship—and these are the things that make sustainable, long, viable, peaceful societies.

—ABIGAIL DISNEY

Very important human strengths that, it seems to me, are absolutely essential to probable survival at this point in history are gendered feminine in this culture. The value on relationships, the value on integrating thought with emotion, a kind of sense that there's more than one story, the search for mutual understanding—these are all traits that in a patriarchy are gendered feminine. . . . If you think historically, this is really about the move from patriarchy to democracy, because in patriarchy it's all about gender, and in democracy, gender is irrelevant—it's really about human qualities.

—CAROL GILLIGAN

Anything and everything is possible when women are brought to the table. . . . There are a lot of biological processes that make women more equipped to handle change. Women experience life as cyclical right in their own bodies, and I think this makes them more adept at going with the flow, adapting, and being able to move from one thing to the next. There is a nurturing aspect to women that is probably hardwired hormonally and is definitely enhanced by our culture. This generally leads us to have a greater sense of compassion. Society also forces women to grow in a way that men aren't required to. Many women have had to and continue to have to work hard to survive, whether juggling life-or-death situations or juggling families and jobs. Women are responsible for managing things and doing them all as well as they possibly can.

—SALLY FIELD

The reason I made women's issues central to American foreign policy was not because I was a feminist, but because we know that societies are more stable if women are politically and economically empowered. Women don't have trouble finding work, but they need to be valued and they need to be part of a legal system. So I did it for a number of reasons, but it makes a difference. I have found it hard to just talk about women's issues—they are *people* issues, and they are very central to how people treat each other.

—MADELEINE ALBRIGHT

Look at the world, and look at how men have driven the warfare, how women are always left picking up the pieces. Women tend to find alternative ways of conflict resolution that are much more helpful than simply going and bombing the hell out of each other. You know, we have playground bullying and we want to find a better way to solve the problem of the bully in the playground apart from physical retaliation, an eye for an eye, et cetera. Why can't that be reflected in the world at large?

—ANNIE LENNOX

There are so many studies done about how there is a women's way of leadership that's different from men's. Some men are more female-like in their leadership, and some women are more male-like, so it's not everyone, but you can generalize to say that women tend to be more inclusive, they tend to listen better, they tend to bring people to consensus, and they also tend to think outside of the box of priorities, because they've been strangers in a strange land, so they're not as acclimated to the priorities that have already been set. So they're not so much on autopilot. They tend to ask why. "Why have we been doing it like this the whole time?" and "We do it a different way." They question the way things have always been done, because they haven't been doing them. This is the same for all minorities. It's uncomfortable, but it's a good idea to get new thinking in.

Some of what keeps us from barging through obstacles is actually a great strength that this society does not honor. It's the value women have, which is: listen to other people, ask for directions, be vulnerable within relationships—meaning, bare your soul, tell your truth, admit your weakness. These are good qualities. I would hate to think that in our race to the top we would let go of some of our most stellar qualities, the very qualities that a new leader needs. This is our big challenge now: to be strong, resolute, not concerned if we're not liked, able to ask for what we want, able to believe that "I know as much as he knows."

How do we remain vulnerable as we race to the top? I don't have the answer, but I know it can be done—as long as we keep saying that it's important.

—ELIZABETH LESSER

As women, we have different values. I call them "feminist values." We believe in sharing, we believe in cooperation, instead of domination and discrimination. So we as women have the values that we need to make our society and our country a better place.

There are still some people unfortunately out there that are not enlightened and they don't realize that women can be great leaders. Let's inform them. Look at all of the history of the world, of the things that women have done to make the world a better place. Let's convince them. And I think now we have probably the best opportunity ever because we've seen that there has been so much hatred that has been thrown out there in our societies, so much discrimination. It's up to us. We, women, have the power. We can do it. We can make it happen.

—DOLORES HUERTA

Women bring not just strong minds but strong hearts and strong souls to every single thing that we do. The wisdom and the engagement and the tenacity that we bring to everything we do can be felt in our work and political life as well. We say that the personal is political, and the political is personal, so there's nothing that we're working on at home or with our families or with our community that is not affected by what's happening on Capitol Hill. So we have to show up in every single place and bring the unique perspective and drive that only a woman can.

—BRITTANY PACKNETT

3

LIVE UNAPOLOGETICALLY

Stand firm in what you know in your heart of hearts. Be exactly who you are, unapologetically and with great passion and positivity.
—Elizabeth Lesser

For so long in our culture, women have been taught or expected to be nice, to conform, to fit in, to be quiet, to acquiesce, and to just generally not ruffle any feathers.

This starts early, since as girls we are often conditioned by society to "please" and be liked. Even now, literally on social media, many girls and young women are growing accustomed to judging their value by the number of likes they might get on one of their Instagram posts. And yet, the goal of being popular or liked at all costs is absolutely antithetical to being able to be an effective leader, since being liked by everyone, all the time, is impossible.

Both women and girls have to feel empowered to speak their minds and make decisions based on their own inner compass of what is right, rather than with a motivation to please others or be liked. In fact, among the remarkable leaders I have been fortunate to interact with or interview, one thing they all have in common is that they simply don't care as much about what other people think. Speaker of the House Nancy Pelosi said as much to me recently, when offering advice to women entering politics. She said you shouldn't worry about what other people say about you because "that's their problem, not yours."

For women to be effective leaders, enact change, and really be successful and happy in life, we need to let go of these cultural constraints and realize that we don't need to please everyone and we don't need to apologize for not doing so. We can begin to change the culture by being true to ourselves, using our voices, not worrying about backlash, and simply being unapologetically and proudly who we are.

The truth is that after so much societal conditioning we have taken in, it can be hard to shrug off caring what other people think or say about us—it takes practice and vigilance. Here are some strategies offered by women who model and practice it themselves.

THREE KEYS TO LIVING UNAPOLOGETICALLY

---

1. BE YOUR AUTHENTIC SELF

Just be what it is that you are, and that is *just fine*. You don't have to be what you're not in any way. Live that and live that fully, and that is where you discover ecstasy. You can't really have ecstasy as something other than yourself.

—ALICE WALKER

I think vulnerability is power. I like vulnerable and open people, and I think when you're that way, you are actually being very brave. By presenting the real truth of yourself, who you really are, you change the molecules in the room.

—AMY POEHLER

Courage is a state of mind, of fearlessness, of being fearless. And we can be this on a daily basis. It takes courage to step out of your skin, to step out of your role, to step out of society's roles for you. Courage is when you dare to be yourself, in whatever ways you want to be—to not be afraid, to just do it.

—LOUNG UNG

Be your authentic self. The best advice I ever got running for office was "Be yourself." Authenticity is everything. Think of what you have to offer and how unique that is.

—NANCY PELOSI

What we all try to do in our lives is amplify our souls—try to be as authentic as we can be and as whole as we can be, regardless of what people think or what society says we should be. We all want to die having lived—having been authentic, whole people. That's the goal.

—JANE FONDA

2. SPEAK YOUR TRUTH

It took me quite a long time to develop a voice, and now that I have it, I am not going to be silent.

—MADELEINE ALBRIGHT

So many people are afraid to speak out; they're afraid to ruffle feathers. But we have to. Every voice counts and that voice needs to be heard. And by not using your voice, you're doing a disservice not only to yourself, but to the community and the world at large. You have a responsibility to all of us. We need your help. I think girls and women are our heroes, and they need to start seeing themselves as our heroes and to come help us out of the mess that we're in.

—JENNIFER SIEBEL NEWSOM

Huge pressures are brought to bear on women to dismiss a truthful voice as "stupid" or to hear it as crazy or to see it as bad or selfish or wrong. We know that voice; it's just, as we start to reach for it or it starts to come up, we've been inducted into a culture that would have us dismiss that voice.

So what happens is the human voice gets shut down—earlier in boys, later in girls—and that voice to me right now is absolutely crucial. The bad news is, there are both psychologically and politically huge forces against listening to that voice. The good news is, that voice is in each of us, and we all know it. It's accessible.

—CAROL GILLIGAN

I was always encouraged to talk in my family. They never told me to be quiet. No one ever said, "Be quiet, Joy." And believe me, I must have irritated them plenty. But, I don't know, they just thought I was amusing or something, and they let me just yak it up. So you don't tell girls to be quiet. Stop telling us to be quiet; we're not going to be quiet.

—JOY BEHAR

You can't please everybody, so you might as well just speak the truth. That's all your job is: to speak the truth. If nothing else, because at least you know that you were authentic to yourself, and at the end of the day, you have to basically answer to yourself, not anybody else. . . .

What's at stake are our basic rights and the things that we hold dear. I don't think we can afford to be silent anymore. I think it is expensive to be quiet sometimes. I think it costs us more to be quiet than it does to speak up.

—LUVVIE AJAYI

If it's not as easy for women to speak our truth, to even know our truth, then the missing ingredient is some sort of inner courage. To first of all believe in the validity of who we are and then speak from it, it takes inner courage.

As a leader in a large organization, I've often been the only woman working with powerful men, especially when I was younger. It really honed in me a courage to go out on a limb and demand to be heard in the only way that I really knew how to speak: from my female voice, the "different voice." Because if we try to speak in a voice that isn't ours, we lose our power.

Sometimes to speak as a woman is to cry and to speak from our emotional, intuitive knowing, as opposed to graphs and charts and vertical lines. And that's scary—that's scary to do—and the fallout from it can be brutal, and then it's scary to go on.

I'm interested in helping women become courageous in being exactly who they are, because the only way to change anything is to do it from your genuine self.

What I've learned over my years in leadership is, first, to trust that what I feel, know, and see is of value. And second, to learn to speak it in such a way that it's listened to and acted on. One of the problems with traditional leadership training programs is that they don't take into account this deep obstacle that many women have: this pervading, yet unconscious feeling within, bolstered by society, that what you have to say really isn't of value. If family and society tell you it's unfeminine to be aggressive, to speak up, to have strong opinions, to take up space, then women won't trust their own voice. To be heard and to be influential, you've got to have a way to sing out with passion and love and self-trust—to sing out your song for everyone to hear. Women leaders are at a disadvantage because we are actually taught not to sing out with strength and conviction.

—ELIZABETH LESSER

We need women to speak up. Share your voice. We live in a moment where communication is so, so important and so, so accessible. You have something to say, and you should say it. We're all listening.

—DONNA KARAN

What I've discovered is that you can be so much more powerful if you're talking from your soul, from your core self. We have to break through silence and speak our truth.

—JANE FONDA

3. DON'T WORRY ABOUT BEING LIKED

As a woman gets more successful, she is less liked by people of both genders, and as a man gets more successful, he does not take a likability hit. . . . I really believe we can change it. I try to teach people about the likability penalty women pay for success, so when they hear, "Oh, this woman's doing a good job, but she's just not well liked by her peers," they have enough sense to question that and ask why.

—SHERYL SANDBERG

Women are culturally taught to seek approval, not disapproval. So as Sheryl Sandberg points out, we have to lean in and not be dependent on being liked as much as the culture has encouraged us to be.

—GLORIA STEINEM

I feel like you can be kind, just, and fair without having to worry about if every single person likes you. You come to a point in life where you just go, "It's none of my business what people think of me. It's my business how I act, and am I acting in a way that I respect? Am I living in my skin?" Life is too short.

—KATHY NAJIMY

All of us know not what is expedient, not what is going to make us popular, not what the policy is—but in truth each of us knows what is the right thing to do. And that's how I am guided.

—MAYA ANGELOU

So much of our lives are spent trying to make someone happy other than ourselves, and the verb "to please" has robbed girls and robbed all of us of our greatest energy and creativity. It has prevented us from taking risks, prevented us from speaking the truth, and prevented us from standing up against tyranny and war and oppression because we're afraid of being exiled. If women believe that they can be free, that they can have a voice, that they can do whatever they want, and that they have the right and the mandate to fight for it, anything can happen. But part of it is breaking through our own sense of limitation and our fear that if we step forward, people won't like us. And I think that's the main thing we really have to break through—our own sense of limitations.

Give voice to what you know to be true, and do not be afraid of being disliked or exiled. That's the hard work of standing up for what you see.

—EVE ENSLER

I feel like if I'm getting a lot of heat directed at me, it makes me feel like I'm probably doing something right. You know, if you're making people feel uncomfortable, it means that you're shaking core beliefs, which is what we're supposed to be doing, which is what we want to do.

—JESSICA VALENTI

Don't be patient and don't wait for someone to ask you and don't think everyone's going to like you, because if you're not pissing someone off, you're probably not doing your job! And that's how change happens, because people are bold and audacious.

—CECILE RICHARDS

4

TAKE RISKS, MAKE MISTAKES, AND PERSIST

My advice to anyone who cares about something is to just not give up. Don't be afraid to fail. Keep fighting. Every time you move the ball forward, you can build on that success.

—Kirsten Gillibrand

When I reflect back on some of my life experiences that didn't go as I planned and at the time I viewed as setbacks, I realize now in hindsight that those were essential course corrections and necessary parts of my journey that have taken me to where I am today.

In order to achieve our goals and dreams, women have to be willing to risk failure and make mistakes—it is practically impossible to make progress toward achieving anything bold without doing so! As Pat Mitchell once pointed out to me, for women to really step into leadership and pursue our lives and our work, "You have to be brave enough to take risks."

And when we do inevitably experience some type of "failure" or rejection or fall, we cannot view it as a setback but rather as an opportunity to learn, grow, and become more resilient, because very often these experiences offer further insight or direction and point us toward what we need to do to achieve our goals. After all, we can't know how much we can truly accomplish unless we're willing to continually push the limits and take chances.

Women have to give ourselves permission not to do everything perfectly. We can often be our own worst critics, and treating ourselves with compassion and understanding while allowing ourselves to make mistakes and stumble along the way is absolutely essential to nurturing our self-esteem and well-being. Only then can we finally learn the invaluable lessons that can help us reach our highest aspirations.

I always go back to my grandmother's advice to me, which was the first time I fell and hurt myself. She said to me, "Honey, at least falling on your face is a forward movement." And that came back to me many times as I failed to get the job or failed to do things perfectly or whatever. You have to be willing to be brave enough to risk falling on your face, to risk failing. Everything we do is about taking risks.

—PAT MITCHELL

Here's one thing that I worry about: we're not willing to make mistakes. We're very nervous about making a wrong move and we worry that if we make the wrong move, then the consequences will mean that we never recover from them. It's okay—in fact, it's better than okay—to make mistakes, really big mistakes sometimes. So I would want to say to young women, "Hey, run for office, even if you think you're going to lose. Take a hard class, even if you're going to get a C in it. Go ahead and follow love, even if it doesn't work out." We need just a little bit of courage to make mistakes, because that strikes me as where all the good stuff happens.

—MELISSA HARRIS-PERRY

How have [my successes and failures] taught me? They *are* me. All my failures and all my successes as a mother and as a daughter and as a professional are me. I am a reflection of all of it. I reach out and sometimes I succeed and sometimes I fail. If I fail or get hurt, I pick myself up.

—SALLY FIELD

We may encounter many defeats, but we must not be defeated. It may even be necessary to encounter the defeat, so that we can know who we are. So that we can see, "Oh, that happened, and I rose. I did get knocked down flat in front of the whole world, and I rose. I didn't run away; I rose right where I'd been knocked down." That's how you get to know yourself. You say, "Hmm . . . I can get up! I have so much courage in me that I have the effrontery, the incredible gall to stand up." That's it. That's how you get to know who you are.

Look what you've already come through! Don't deny it. You've already come through some things, which are very painful. You have gone through some pain; it cost you something, and you've come through it. So at least look at that. Have the sense to look at yourself and say, "Well, wait a minute. I'm stronger than I thought I was." We need to not be in denial about what we've done, what we've come through. It will help us if we all do that.

—MAYA ANGELOU

It's not as much a matter of winning or losing but the fact that you're in the arena, you know what it takes, the ups and downs, and that you get up and you do it again and you learn from that experience. The give-and-take and the team playing—it all contributes to addressing all dimensions of your experiences and life's experiences. There's no substitute for that. Those are assets and qualities that transcend in your life, for the remainder of your life. You know what it's like—you're down one day, and you have to get up the next. So you lose one game, but you know if you come back you can win the next time. That's important to experience, the winning and losing. It's the give-and-take in life—those things happen, and you can rebound from them and succeed.

—OLYMPIA SNOWE

Just do it. You can't know if you will succeed or fail if you don't even try. And if you've got the courage to feel strongly about something—women are very strong—and if you believe in something and you care about your country, then you ought to have the courage to step out and do it. You might get out and discover a whole new world open to you that you never knew existed.

—CAROL MOSELEY BRAUN

Don't let people tell you what you can't do. If it's something that you really want to do, you're going to have to have the fortitude to just know, even when there are naysayers, that you're not going to listen to them.

—KELLY AYOTTE

I don't even think of my life in terms of obstacles. You know, the fact that I was born in a city that had no democratic government— I mean, we had no local government, no democracy. Or that I was a black child that went to segregated schools, because the DC schools were segregated until the '54 decision. Or that I was a woman. I have never considered any of those things to be obstacles. They're the things that give you fight. I just think if you sit down and count the obstacles, you're counting yourself out. I didn't think I had any obstacles. I just had to do it.

—ELEANOR HOLMES NORTON

I am amazed by the strength of women. And the more they are being put down, the stronger they are. Women's strength just never ceases to amaze me and to inspire me.

—DIANE VON FURSTENBERG

Sometimes these blows are so severe that you just think, *Well, it's not about whether I deserved it—it's just that that's what's happening.* And since that's what's happening, what do you do with it? As the years have gone on, I have really gotten to that place where I do say to myself, "Well, wow—I bet I'm going to learn something pretty amazing right here, because this is so painful or this is so strange." And that has been true!

—ALICE WALKER

5

BE CONFIDENT AND COURAGEOUS

I always push the envelope. I don't want to be caught in the same place for very long and any time I feel frightened of doing something, that usually means I better get in there and do it.

—Sally Field

It takes courage to put yourself out there and be a leader. It takes believing in yourself and building confidence so that others will believe in you, too, and follow your lead. Yet as women, we have societal pressures and stereotypes working against us. Confident, ambitious women are often portrayed by the media and society as "unlikable," and we have so many forces that, throughout our life, whittle away at our self-esteem and encourage us to be submissive.

Even as children, as Sheryl Sandberg once told me, girls who speak their minds or advocate for themselves are deemed "bossy" in a negative way, rather than being commended for showing leadership skills. These subliminal messages and influences get baked into our psyche early on—and they have lasting effects. The result is that while women frequently face institutional obstacles, women can also have internal glass ceilings that keep them from pursuing leadership positions or going after what they want. Oftentimes, this is because of internalized sexism and low self-worth.

But women will never be able to achieve parity in leadership or assume our rightful place at the tables of influence without being empowered and comfortable to be confident and courageous—to have ambitious goals, advocate for ourselves, follow our dreams, and ask for (or demand!) a seat at the table, whether in the corporate world, politics, or in any influential sphere we envision for ourselves.

When I interviewed legendary poet and activist Maya Angelou, who overcame intense personal and societal challenges in her life to become an incredibly powerful voice in our culture, she emphasized to me that she thought courage was "the most important of all the virtues." In order to create the urgent and important changes we want to see in the world, we need women to step confidently and courageously into their power—and not be afraid to use it. Here are some inspiring quotes and strategies to embolden us along the way.

FIVE KEYS TO BEING CONFIDENT AND COURAGEOUS

1. DON'T DOUBT YOURSELF

One thing that I hear from women of all ages is a lot of self-doubt. And [I share] with them my own experience. I didn't go through any political training, but I understood what the most important qualification was: a sense of purpose and motivation toward serving others. The rest you can learn. [If] you're rooted and grounded in understanding and knowing why you're doing what you're doing, then you'll have the correct perspective to be able to persevere and let the arrows that are shot at you bounce off you; it gives you that protective armor.

—TULSI GABBARD

Don't doubt. Don't doubt what you know.

—KERRY WASHINGTON

You have to believe in who you are and what difference you can make. Have confidence in the contribution that you can make. You believe, you care, you have confidence—and that's not to be egotistical. It's just to be confident.

—NANCY PELOSI

2. BE TRUE TO YOURSELF

I think being exactly yourself is really important. And I think you should own your ambition and be who you are and not be afraid of that. I think for me, as a young woman, I was tentative in a lot of things. I was unsure. I didn't embrace all my ambition. I was more tentative than I should have been. I was definitely more fearful than I should have been. Women need to have the confidence to be who they want to be and know that they're different and that's a good thing.

—KIRSTEN GILLIBRAND

Women just have to have the confidence, taking inventory of what they have accomplished, whether it's being a mom, being a teacher, being a small-business woman, being in the military—whatever it happens to be, whatever combination of experiences—[to] place a gold star on all of it. Be proud of it.

—NANCY PELOSI

Lord knows it's scary to step out in this culture, isn't it? It's scary to take the road less traveled. It's scary to walk into a room and say, "I'd like to be the leader of this." Who you decide you are and want to be comes from your experiences and how you process them and how you believe your life should go. I think that's all really important. It's really hard to go and lead if you don't know who you are.

—MARIA SHRIVER

There's a saying that says, "To thine own self be true." I really think there's so much more to that than meets the ear or meets the eye. I just think you really have to know who you are—come to terms with that, accept that and love that, and understand your talents, what your gifts may be, and how to develop them.

So I think if you're comfortable with yourself and know yourself, you're going to shine and radiate and other people are going to be drawn to you. And by doing that I think you can do a lot for people; you'll have a lot of help because people want to be around you.

—DOLLY PARTON

I always try to say to people, "Find out your own potentiality. Don't look to other people and put them on a pedestal; it's pointless. Find your own strength. Look to your own strengths and weaknesses, and be your own self."

—ANNIE LENNOX

3. ACKNOWLEDGE YOUR FEAR

If we are waiting for our fear to abate, if we're waiting for the fear to go away for us to do the stuff that's important, we're never going to step up. We're never going to stand up. We cannot wait for fear to go away because it's like waiting for breathing to go away. It's like waiting for thinking to go away. These are core human parts of us. So courage is not the absence of fear. It's not about *not* feeling fear. It's not about conquering fear. It's about having the capacity to notice your fear, to notice it with compassion because you're feeling fearful about something—and something that matters to you.

So we want to notice our fear with compassion. We want to notice our fear with curiosity: What is this fear trying to say to me? What is it specifically that I am scared of here? What is this fear trying to tell me? So courage is about being able to notice our fear with curiosity and with compassion and still choose to take steps in the direction of our values.

We know that we are reaching levels of social change, gender change, equity, more value-based ways of being, not when we are not feeling fear but when we're taking steps in the direction of our values; that often feels fearful, and that's normal.

—SUSAN DAVID

Being brave is not being unafraid but feeling the fear and doing it anyway. When you feel fear, try using it as a signal that something really important is about to happen.

—GLORIA STEINEM

4. DON'T BACK DOWN

Be passionate about what you believe in and do not be afraid to stand alone, because you may find yourself in a position one day where you have to stand alone. That doesn't mean it's easy; it isn't. But if you know that you feel strongly about a certain position and certain values or a certain view, and if you believe you're right, then you should be able to stand alone.

—OLYMPIA SNOWE

We need courage, we need conviction, we need people that are willing to risk their comfort, risk their status, risk potential reward to stand firmly on the foundation of whatever principle they believe in—at the same time, always remembering that none of us have exclusivity to the truth or exclusivity to what's right. We have to maintain a willingness to reach out and engage those that disagree with us and maintain an openness to argument.

—GAVIN NEWSOM

When you talk about people who do things that people perceive as really courageous, most of the time what motivates them is not the risk that they're looking at of what might happen that would be really, really disastrous for them, but what's the importance of what it is you're trying to achieve.

So for me, when I think about the [Clarence Thomas] hearing, what motivated me to do it was bigger than the consequences of doing it. . . . I think there's someplace in your conscience that says, "If I don't act, then I will have been a part of something that I don't want to live with." I would have been moving away from something and turning my back on something.

—ANITA HILL

Over the years I began to understand through a long, hard process that my instincts and vision were valid. The work I have done to gain confidence in my own voice has been so important. I learned how to speak in a way that will be heard and to know when not to back down, when to hold my ground.

—ELIZABETH LESSER

Have you ever been at the table at a meeting or something where you'll say something great, and nobody will pick it up, and two seconds later a man will say the same thing? And they'll say, "What a great idea!" And you're like, "What? I just said that." I've only concluded lately that the reason they didn't salute the woman when she said it is because they weren't listening. So you have to make sure they hear you.

—NANCY PELOSI

Martin Luther King Jr. said, "Our lives begin to end on the day we stop talking about things that matter most." There is a perverse comfort zone to living a small life. For women, that zone has to do with the fact that we're less likely to be challenged, we're less likely to be criticized, we're less likely to be called angry or strident, if we simply go along and acquiesce to the prevailing patterns of thought and behavior. But as Krishnamurti said, "It is no measure of health to be well adjusted to a profoundly sick society." It's not as though life now is easy and showing up for the world is hard. No—the way many of us are living now is diseased and dysfunctional, and showing up for the world is one of the ways we heal. . . . It's time to show up in a way we've never shown up before.

—MARIANNE WILLIAMSON

It's a courageous act to just be with whatever is happening at the moment—all of it, the difficult as well as the wonderful.

—EILEEN FISHER

Women have always been courageous. They are the bravest of the brave! They are always fearless when protecting their children, and in the last century they have been fearless in the fight for their rights.

—ISABEL ALLENDE

5. GO FOR IT

There is no one way to [find the courage to face your fear]. I think it just comes from knowing, acknowledging the fact that it is scary but then kind of taking a deep breath, swallowing hard, and just doing whatever that is anyway. There is no easy way—just do it. It's just one of those things that comes with the fortitude of like, "Okay, I have to do it. So I am just going to acknowledge the fact that this is how I am feeling about it, but it is not going to stop me." I am really trying to encourage people to do what feels scary . . . encouraging people to just tell the truth.

—LUVVIE AJAYI

I would encourage us to try our best to develop courage. It's the most important of all the virtues, because without courage, you can't practice any other virtue consistently. You can be anything erratically—kind, fair, true, generous, all that. But to be that thing time after time, you need courage.

We need to develop courage, and we need to develop it in small ways first. Because we wouldn't go and say, "I'll pick up this hundred-pound weight" without knowing our capacity. So we need to say, "Oh, I'll start by picking up a five-pound weight, then a ten-pound weight, then a twenty-five-pound, and sooner or later I'll be able to pick up a one-hundred-pound weight." And I think that's true with courage.

—MAYA ANGELOU

If you're just willing to hang in there and be tough and follow your dreams with commitment and courage, you can do anything.

—KAY BAILEY HUTCHISON

When I first started stand-up comedy, I think part of my motivation for getting into it was that I felt powerless as a woman in this society. I was becoming invisible. I was already thirty-nine. I was just becoming more and more invisible, and I was like, "I have things to say. I have to do it." As hard as that was, I got up on that stage with a microphone in my hand, and I went there.

—JOY BEHAR

If you want something and you've never had it before, you're going to have to do something you've never done before in order to get it.

—TIFFANY DUFU

Be open to opportunities. See the opportunities when they appear, and seize opportunities.

—ANA NAVARRO

My career advice is just *do* the thing; don't talk about the thing. Whatever it is, do it. Commit to as much time doing it as you do talking about doing it, and that might just get you somewhere.

—AMY POEHLER

6

KNOW YOUR WORTH

My call to action is stay focused and be tenacious. Women have to be tenacious and tough and have a thick skin. They should spend their time focusing on fixing the big things, such as pay inequity, inclusion in decision-making, and getting themselves to the top, as opposed to near the top.

—Tina Brown

Two personal stories on knowing your worth come to mind from my encounters with one of my most important role models and life mentors: Gloria Steinem. Gloria has given me many powerful words of wisdom over the years. At a fundraiser she graciously hosted at her home for my nonprofit organization Feminist.com, where there was a lot of talk about us habitually working on a "shoestring budget," she encouraged me to "ask for what I need" and pushed me to make sure I got compensated for the work I was doing. And at the launch event for my first book, *Daring to Be Ourselves*, which was also a celebration of Feminist .com's fifteen-year anniversary, I will always remember when Gloria put her arm around me, looked me in the eyes, and told me I should feel proud of this moment. I deflected her compliment by saying I was really just a conduit for helping promote other amazing thought leaders and organizations, but she gently stopped me and reminded me not to defer it outward, but to take this moment in, give myself credit, and value my accomplishments. Asking for what we need and knowing our value are two messages many women and girls need today!

Women knowing our worth has widespread implications for achieving gender equality. There is a lot of research that shows that women tend to doubt themselves more than men and don't advocate for themselves as much as they should. For example, women often don't think they are qualified enough to run for office, don't advocate for a raise or for a promotion, or don't stand up to question their company's pay structure if there is an imbalance. To be our own best advocates, for our sake as well as for gender equality more generally, women need to trust in what we have to offer: our unique talents and our potential—to know our worth and then make sure we (and those around us) are recognized and compensated accordingly.

As we strive for gender equality, women have to advocate for ourselves, whether it is believing in our visions, articulating what we uniquely bring to a job or project, negotiating for a raise, or raising funding for our own ventures or political campaigns—it all starts with us believing in ourselves.

Women are usually hired on performance and men are hired on potential. It is very important that when companies are hiring they start thinking about women's potential, not just their performance, because they always keep us back that way. Like if a woman is going to get on a board, what kind of experience does she have? Well, 75 percent of men that are on boards are rookies. They haven't been on any board either, but no one ever questions that. So women have to stand up and remind them, "Look, I have potential. I can do this."

Think about your potential—what you've been given. Practice your strengths. Know your strengths because, just like in sports, we practice our strengths every single day, and we make our weaknesses adequate. If you have a strength, go for it. Zone in on that and that will help you decide where you are going to go.

—BILLIE JEAN KING

I take seriously this notion when I talk to young women about, "Do you know what the person sitting next to you is making? Because nine times out of ten, they're making more than you are, doing the same work." [I was talking to] a young friend who had just gotten a great raise and we had a conversation about pay equity, and so I said, "When you replaced the guy in your job, what was the pay discrepancy?" She said, "Well, he made about seventy thousand dollars more than I did, and I was doing most of his work."

It's in the unladylike category to be talking about money and asking about money, but . . . you have to feel that you're worthy of it. You have to know that it is not right and fair, even though that's the way it's always been done, and somebody sitting next to you or somebody that you replaced was making two salaries more than you're making. Money is a piece of this machinery, unfortunately. So until they change that, this is the part that you have to learn and master.

—CAROL JENKINS

Money, unfortunately, is not in the hands of women. If you look at salary disparities, is it any wonder that we have the wealth gap that we have in the United States of America for women, whereby white women own thirty-three cents on the white man's one dollar of wealth, and African American and Latina women own one and two cents on the white man's one dollar of wealth? We have a long way to go.

We know that we still don't pay our women enough. We know that we aren't paying women equitably and reinforcing and providing security for them in their careers. And let's not forget that we as a society don't have the policies in place that would enable working women to raise children while having a very prolific career. So we have a lot of work to do when it comes to paid leave, universal preschool, and childcare.

I think there's more we can do, and it requires men of consciousness in leadership advocating for real systemic change, and it requires more women in leadership, such that we can really create a huge paradigm shift. . . . It's going to require more and more of us to demand that it happen—demand the equal pay—and it requires the allies to have our back.

—JENNIFER SIEBEL NEWSOM

Gender parity matters because it's the only way to actually have anything be fair. Whether you're talking about in government, corporate structure, families—parity means that all sides are being considered. And it's not just a moral obligation, it's also a financial imperative. Because if you want to run a successful company, successful companies are diverse. The more diversity you have on your executive board and at high levels in the company, the better the company does. So not only do we have a moral duty to make sure that everyone is being fairly represented, but we're talking about incredible return on investment here as well.

—SOPHIA BUSH

I care about equity and equality because people deserve to have their full rights acknowledged, and you need to live in a life and walk in a world where you're fully acknowledged and actualized, and you can't do that if you don't have an equal playing field.

—TARANA BURKE

Women have had to really fight to reduce systemic and institutional barriers on all fronts. When you look at the pay inequity at this point and the gap in terms of how much a woman makes versus a man—we're still fighting that battle. Our struggle for equal rights is not over, and I think that's reflected in all levels of government and in the private sector.

—BARBARA LEE

Gender equality is critical because right now we live in an unequal society that actually values the lives and the contributions of men over women. And as long as we have a hierarchy of human value in this country, we're actually never going to realize freedom. We're never going to realize opportunity. Achieving gender equality is a step toward achieving a society where we undo the hierarchies of human value that have created unsafe workplaces, undignified workplaces. What's at stake is all the creativity and the contributions and the ideas and the huge amount of human potential that we leave on the table by suppressing and devaluing women.

—AI-JEN POO

We need to be seen, all over the place. We need to be seen as well as heard. It's not sufficient to say, "Well, we are here, and we deserve." If we really think that the majority of women in the world are always in the kitchen and in the kindergarten and in the places just to look after the young and the men, then we do ourselves and everybody a disservice. Because women offer so much more than it would seem we offer. It would seem we offer kindness and the chance to be cared for and nursed in more ways than just medical. And I think that the whole country needs to know that women are much smarter—we're more than that. We're that and more than that.

—MAYA ANGELOU

Any insistence on equal pay is crucial and any redefinition of work to include caregiving work so that it also has an economic value, at least at replacement level, that's crucial.

—GLORIA STEINEM

On the economic side, if we are going to out-innovate, out-compete, and out-educate other countries, our competitors, we are only going to succeed if women are leading the way. And that's largely because women are now graduating with more than 50 percent of advanced degrees, more than 50 percent of college degrees, and women-owned and minority-owned businesses are the fastest-growing sector within small businesses. So if we had equal pay in this country, you could raise the GDP by up to 9 percent. Because women-owned businesses are so fast growing, if they had the same access to capital—women start businesses with eight times less capital than men—we would see greater economic growth. With women's participation in the economy, in economic and political decision-making, we would have a better result. And we frankly just need women right now to be part of these decisions.

—KIRSTEN GILLIBRAND

Anyone you talk to in organizations that work to get more women into politics, they'll tell you that women don't run for office at the same levels that men do because they're taught to think that they're not qualified. So if a city council seat comes up and you ask a guy who has the same experience that a woman has, "Are you qualified?" he'll say, "Absolutely!" You talk to the woman and she'll say, "Well, no, I don't think so. I don't think I'm the right kind of person" or "I don't have the right kind of experience." So we have to start with building up confidence and just getting women to want to put their names in the hat.

—JESSICA VALENTI

As I tell my students at Georgetown, "Visibility is viability." If you're not visible in society and you're not out there, people don't know you exist. . . . Often we don't push ourselves to go out there. We have a culture where women still don't self-promote. It's important to go out there. I have to tell you the truth: it's not easy to do that . . . but it's worth it. When I push, I push. You've got to self-promote, and I know that's hard for some women, and some of them simply don't like to do it, but think about [men]— they will self-promote in a nanosecond. I think we have to do self-promotion. . . . What are we waiting for?

—DONNA BRAZILE

I was taught as a young girl that it was impolite to talk about money. I was taught that it's not something you inquired about and that it would be a sign of failure if you needed to ask someone for money. Well, clearly you cannot be successful in modern politics if you do not get very comfortable with talking about money and the notion of asking complete strangers for checks with commas in them. This is as essential to success as breathing, especially in a race like president of the United States. And to get to be a candidate for president of the United States, you have to demonstrate your ability at other offices, and that obviously entails fundraising. So that skill was, and still is, [a factor]—whether it is the reluctance of women to be donors or the reluctance of women to "close" on fundraising.

—CLAIRE McCASKILL

Women: know your power, and know you're needed. Be yourself and be confident in the fact that what you have to offer is unique.

—NANCY PELOSI

Q&A WITH TINA BROWN ON EQUAL PAY AND WOMEN RISING TO THE TOP

Women really have to take stock of and seek advice on the issue of where they are in being compensated and how.

—Tina Brown

Tina Brown is an award-winning writer and editor, founder of the Women in the World Summit, and president and CEO of Tina Brown Live Media. Between 1979 and 1998, she was the editor of Tatler, Vanity Fair, *and* The New Yorker. *Her 2007 biography of the Princess of Wales,* The Diana Chronicles, *topped the* New York Times *bestseller list. In 2008 she founded The Daily Beast, which won the Webby Award for Best News Site in 2012 and 2013. Queen Elizabeth honored her in 2000 as a Commander of the Order of the British Empire (CBE) for her services to overseas journalism, and in 2007 she was inducted into the US Magazine Editors' Hall of Fame. She founded the Women in the World Summit in 2010 and launched Tina Brown Live Media in 2014 to expand Women in the World internationally. She is also the author of* The Vanity Fair Diaries, *which chronicles her years as the editor in chief of* Vanity Fair.

MARIANNE SCHNALL: This feels like a very fertile moment that we're in where there is this unprecedented awareness and engagement among women, who are stepping up in all kinds of ways. How do you see this moment that we are in for women?

TINA BROWN: I think it's a watershed and tipping point in every way. And the thing about my Women in the World Summit is we've been amplifying these issues, really, since 2010 when we began. We were kind of lonely in that moment, and very early on we found it hard to get the sense of "this was a movement," which is actually what I felt: that a global movement was beginning. What is exciting here is that this movement has come full circle and we're now seeing America galvanized by Trump, galvanized by #MeToo, actually pressing forward and getting very real indeed about ending discrimination against women.

There are a lot of issues that have been discussed for years and years, like pay equity or sexual harassment, but they haven't had this pointed, purposeful, really amplified response that we're getting now.

Equal pay is one thing where you're seeing that women are just saying, "Enough! We're really going to make this happen now." We had the amazing Carrie Grace come to the Women in the World Summit—[she] led the pay equity flurry at the BBC. They offered her a big raise for being China bureau chief and she said, "I don't want the raise; I want equity with the male bureau chief," because she was a very distinguished foreign correspondent. And when she found out that it wasn't equity, it was just a raise, she just said, "No thanks, not taking it. I'll just go back to the newsroom and resign from the bureau chief." She winds up being a great national hero for women in the gender equity issue; she testifies in the parliament. Every BBC anchor came out to support her.

We're seeing now a move toward making pay inequity illegal. England is moving toward making it illegal. In England now, companies are being required to talk about transparency in terms of pay. That has been happening in the US, but of course Trump rolled that back last year when he said companies were not expected, in fact, to reveal their gender makeup in terms of pay distribution. We're seeing a huge amount of energy on this, and it's really real.

MS: **Have you experienced this in your career as well?**

TB: I had my own battles to get myself properly compensated, and I wrote about it in my book *The Vanity Fair Diaries*. I turned the magazine around and turned it into a commercial juggernaut, and I discovered that I wasn't being paid as much as the male editor at *GQ*. It took hiring a major agent lawyer to go in to actually get me a completely different pay structure where I was given a million-dollar bonus for what I had accomplished.

MS: **What can women do to help shift things?**

TB: One of my feelings is that women really have to take stock of and seek advice on the issue of where they are in being compensated and how. One of the things we saw that Carrie Grace talks about at the BBC is the support of other women. Strength in numbers is incredibly important. Other women at BBC coming out on her behalf was a very important aspect. Women have to be supportive of one another. If a company is not doing something right for women, they need to be active and they need to be informed.

MS: **In addition to the challenge of equal pay, we see that the percentage of women in top positions in the corporate world, in media, and in politics is still so far from parity.**

TB: One of the things that blows my mind is there are all these women stuck on the COO level, and there was recently a survey where you had to name a major female leader in tech, and the majority of the responders answered "Siri." Siri! Which made me laugh and cry. Siri and Alexa were the two names that came up just because there aren't many [women leaders in tech]. There are a ton of women stuck at that COO or CFO level, but they're not making it to the top level. How do we change that? At this moment, it's pushing, it's really pushing. . . . It's really important because we need diversity of opinion and approach.

Look at that cabinet picture of Donald Trump discussing Syria with all those men. Not only men, but all white men, fifty-six and up. I'm thinking, *How can you be the ones determining the fate of America that looks so terribly different from you right now in its makeup? Why do we want to keep hearing your retro take on the world and where it should be going?*

MS: **Why do you feel diversity is so important?**

TB: I want to see diversity across the board—in political opinion, gender, race, age. It's really important to have that or you're going to make terrible mistakes. We saw it in the financial crisis in 2008. We saw it in the Iraq War, how a cabinet of very high-testosteroned men took us down the wrong path. We've also seen that companies that have women on the board statistically do better than the ones that don't. There has to be a better mix. It's not just some heartstrings thing, like, "Oh, let's make sure women are here just because it's fair." It makes better sense since women are half the world.

7

GET CLEAR ABOUT WHAT "SUCCESS" MEANS TO YOU

Success is not what you have. It is loving what you do.
—Claire McCaskill

One of the most fundamental rights that the feminist movement has fought for is for women to have and make their own choices. Not choices that are dictated to us by societal conditioning or by other people in our lives, but the choices that are right for us. That can often be hard for many women to even discern, since we may have internalized so many other voices that we've lost touch with our own. We need to establish an honest relationship with ourselves and prioritize time for reflection, so we truly know what it is that makes us feel happy and fulfilled; what it means to us, personally, to live a meaningful life and pursue our true calling.

In this day and age, where many of our institutions are being turned upside down and societal assumptions are being questioned, we need to look freshly at what "success" really means to us. The things that are often associated with success in our society—enormous material wealth, fame, recognition, power—

are not only unachievable for most of us but also do not necessarily lead to happiness and fulfillment. I have interviewed many
wealthy celebrities, from Oprah to Natalie Portman and more,
and they often report that their fulfillment doesn't come from
their fame or wealth at all. Instead, it comes from their advocacy
work, giving back, and being of service to others.

I believe we should redefine success as not only what we
achieve in our careers but also prioritizing things that help give
us a good quality of life—including our health and well-being, our
time spent with our families and special people in our community,
time to support or advocate for causes we care about, and time for
ourselves to rest and reflect.

We also need to realize that there isn't just one measure of
success—it can mean different things to different people. What
does having a successful life mean to you?

There is the obvious power that comes with money or success. But there's also personal power that comes from someone working hard on his or her own internal process—the kind of power we talk about as "finding your voice." It requires you to turn within on a daily basis and not leave any leaf unturned as you discover what it really means to be alive.

—SALLY FIELD

"We are linked, not ranked" was the paradigm of societies for most of human history, and still is of some, and that is the circle, not the pyramid. Viewing the world as linked, not ranked, is profoundly different from viewing it in a hierarchical way, which causes you to label everyone with their place in the hierarchy. What we experience in our childhoods that comes to seem normal, or even inevitable, is that if you are placed in a hierarchy, you probably are immediately anxious about going further down, and you're striving to go further up, so your energies get placed into becoming "more than," or at least not becoming "less than," instead of becoming "part of."

—GLORIA STEINEM

I've been undergoing a great personal and spiritual transformation, and I realized that I had to tear my whole old life down and build it the way that I want it, the way that *I* want my life. So I've been working on that, and that has also turned into building my business the way that I want it. And I realized that I was afraid to handle my own business because I didn't like the way the businesspeople around me were. I was like, "That's the way you do business? That's how you have to be? I don't want to do that." But I realized that I had the opportunity to do business in an ethical way. It's just taking a chance, but it feels good.

—INDIA.ARIE

Still there are days that I feel like a total loser, and I think that every successful person feels that way. You just use it as fuel.

—DIANE VON FURSTENBERG

There's a saying and a song that says, "A man can make money, but money cannot make a man," and there's so much truth in that. You can make all the money in the world, but if you're not happy, you're not a success. So I really measure success in how you deal with the money you make, how you give back.

—DOLLY PARTON

Women need to follow their hearts. It's okay for a woman to lean in. It's also okay for a woman to lean back, if that's what she wants. I think women need to follow their hearts and their minds and not conform to social pressures. And I think we also need to be acutely aware of opportunities when they arise and seize them with both hands.

—ANA NAVARRO

You already have everything you need to be successful. Though I remember spending a lot of time trying to reach outside of myself in order to acquire things that I thought that I needed, now in hindsight, the things that had made me most successful, the things that are my capital, the things that are my highest value, are things that I had all along. And it's so ironic, but you've already got it. You are everything that you need, as opposed to operating from this feeling of inadequacy, as if we're not enough.

—TIFFANY DUFU

The myth of the rugged individualism, the "pull yourselves up by your bootstraps" mentality, breeds this belief that success achieved alone is sweeter than success achieved as a group. Says who? Women, we have to debunk this myth for all girls. This myth raises an "us" against "them" mentality: "If I am going to succeed, then you can't." This myth fosters the idea of finite power and finite position and finite jobs and career opportunities. Why must we all be chasing after that one position? Why can't we create more positions for each other? Why not create five more companies and have five other positions? This myth goes against women's natural talents and abilities as connectors, supporters, networkers, and team players. We have to debunk it immediately!

—LOUNG UNG

We have to remember that the culture still prevailing in many workplaces women are trying to make their way into was created by men, in a workplace culture dominated by men. For far too long, we have equated success with working around the clock, driving yourself into the ground, sleep deprivation, and burnout. This culture is certainly harmful to men, too, but it's women who suffer the most from it—both because women process stress differently and because even when women succeed at work, they're still doing the lion's share of the work at home, too. It's a model of success that's not working for women, and, really, it's not working for men, either.

Women are paying an even higher price than men for their participation in [this] work culture. That is one reason why so many talented women, with impressive degrees working in high-powered jobs, end up abandoning their careers when they can afford to. Women in highly stressful jobs have a nearly 40 percent increased risk of heart disease and heart attacks compared with their less-stressed colleagues and a 60 percent greater risk for type two diabetes—a link that does not exist for men, by the way.

Over time our society's notion of success has been reduced to money and power. In fact, at this point, success, money, and power have practically become synonymous in the minds of many. This idea of success can work, or at least appear to work, in the short term. But over the long term, money and power by themselves are like a two-legged stool: you can balance on it for a while, but eventually you're going to topple over.

More and more people—very successful people—are toppling over. To live the lives we truly want and deserve, and not just the lives we settle for, we need a third metric, a third measure of success that goes beyond the two metrics of money and power. [We need to] make room in our definition of success for well-being, wisdom, wonder, compassion, and giving, and to move from knowing what we need to do to actually doing it.

Women have to lead the way in changing how our workplaces are structured and how we define success—both for their sake and for the sake of successful men who desperately need to learn how to lean back. The world desperately needs it.

Remember that while there will be plenty of signposts along your path directing you to make money and climb up the ladder, there will be almost no signposts reminding you to stay connected to the essence of who you are, to take care of yourself along the way, to reach out to others, to pause to wonder, and to connect to that place from which everything is possible.

—ARIANNA HUFFINGTON

It's been so interesting, the language that's caught on, this "lean in" from Sheryl Sandberg. It's fabulous. I love the metaphor of it, but a glaring omission from the whole concept of leaning in is, What are we leaning in to? Why would I want to lean in so deeply, with so much fervor and time, to something that is at the root of so many of our problems? Why do I want to lean in to a workweek that is so crushing to family? Why should I encourage young women to lean in to a corporate structure where there's no maternity leave to speak of, no paternity leave to speak of? I am not just interested in women being paid as much as men; I'm also interested in [what they're being] paid for. What are we doing this for? If it's just to be equal in a system that is sort of akin to the *Titanic*, I don't want to lean in to the *Titanic*. I want to get the hell out of the *Titanic* and lean in to something of my own creation and encourage other people to lean out and rebuild. So that's the revolutionary in me. I realize that it's also critical that we lean in to the institutions we already have and make change from within. I'm not just throwing this whole message out, but I'm asking that as we lean in, we also try to create more humane structures that honor aspects of life other than money and power, and that we create systems that support the beauty of families and the earth.

As we do this leaning in and gaining our voice and toughening our aggression muscles, all of this is really important, but at the same time, we also have to try to keep our hearts open, our femaleness, and whether it's by nature or nurture doesn't even really matter anymore. Females do tend to be more attentive to others, with a more nurturing spirit, a longer view of what's helpful to multiple generations down the line. We have to stay attentive to those values that we have honed over millennia by being keepers of the family and keepers of the heart, so we can become more aggressive, more strategic, less concerned about whether people like us, and at the same time, we can stay centered in our feeling function, be proud to be emotional creatures, and hone the multi-intelligence that lives in every human being: intelligence of the heart, intelligence of the body, of the spirit—not just these mechanistic intelligences of rationality. We can lean in, lean out, and stand up, all at the same time.

—ELIZABETH LESSER

8

CONSIDER RUNNING FOR OFFICE

There is nothing more wholesome for America, for our politics, for our government, for any walk of life than the increased participation of women in government and in politics. When women succeed, America succeeds. We know this to be an absolute fact in our country.

—Nancy Pelosi

Many women remember a time when running for office seemed like a somewhat rare and obscure career path, one that we were rarely encouraged to pursue. Yet ever since the election of Donald Trump and the Women's March, and in the wake of #MeToo and women looking to have their voices heard, we are experiencing a sea change—women are running, and winning, in record numbers. In the 2018 midterm elections, we achieved historic milestones in terms of the most women ever serving in Congress, set records for women of color and LGBTQ candidates, and saw a slew of other historic firsts, including the first Native American women, the first Muslim women, and the youngest female ever elected to Congress. We witnessed a democracy making strides in becoming as representative as the people it aims to serve.

And yet, despite the progress, we are still far from equity: women make up only 23.7 percent of Congress, only nine out of fifty governors are women, and the US ranks seventy-fifth in the world in terms of women's political representation.

With all the many serious problems we face in this country, we need women's voices and visions at the table, to share our essential insights, stories, solutions, and perspectives. As Nicholas Kristof once told me, more women in US politics "isn't going to just benefit the women of America, it is going to benefit all of America."

So why run? And what advice do women who have walked this path, like Senators Kirsten Gillibrand and Olympia Snowe, and glass-ceiling breakers like twice-elected Speaker of the House Nancy Pelosi, have to offer? Read on for their motivating words of encouragement and guidance.

For someone who's thinking about [running for office], this is what I would say: "Do it. Run." These campaigns, they are tough business, but they're not impossible. And the good, I swear, outweighs the bad. You meet the most amazing people on the campaign trail, you get support from people that you didn't even imagine. And when you get there, the truth is you really do make so much difference for so many people, every day—whether you're in Congress, in the Senate, in the state House, or in the city council—every day you make a difference for somebody, and that's a pretty important piece of what our democracy is about. It's well worth it to take it on.

—STEPHANIE SCHRIOCK

I really think women should be much more excited about a career in elective office. It's a tough business, yes, but most are, and there is an incredible upside. You have a real chance to see and touch things you've been able to change that have made a positive impact on people's lives. I just don't know that it gets any better than that.

And it *is* achievable. I really hope that women aspire to holding elective office. Our country really needs it. . . . It's very important because the more voices, the more different voices, that are involved in public policy, the more sound the public policy is going to be. And frankly, our system of government depends on the acceptance of Americans, that they are being represented in an effective way. So the more Washington reflects how our country actually looks, the more confidence the American people are going to have in it, and therefore our democracy will continue to be the strongest in the world.

—CLAIRE McCASKILL

If you don't strive for a seat at the table, you can't complain about what is decided there.

—TINA BROWN

Every time that women have made progress, typically it's because some woman stepped up and stood up and said, "You know what? This has to change." The progress we've seen in our lifetime happened because of women who dared, women of courage—women like Olympia Snowe and Pat Schroeder and others. Because they spoke up and we got Title IX, because they spoke up and they were able to change the Family and Medical Leave Act, they were able to make advancements on so many other fronts, like assuring that women had access to credit cards. So it's important that women continue to see that when women run, they make a difference in our lives.

—DONNA BRAZILE

I am constantly telling the women in my classes that they should consider running for office, mostly because what we know is that when men are talented and when men are smart and when men show some leadership, it's hard for them to even get to college without someone, at some point, asking them, "Hey, have you ever thought about running for office? Man, you would be a great president." Even as little tiny boys, right? It turns out that we don't have those same kinds of standard messages for girls. So if a woman is very talented and she shows a lot of interest in politics, we tend to say things like "Good job" or "Here's an A on your paper," but we don't tend to say, "Hey, have you ever thought about running for office?"

—MELISSA HARRIS-PERRY

I do think that women are uniquely qualified for leadership. And it is very rewarding to make a difference—to do something that you know makes a difference in quality of life is the reward. There's a lot that's hard about public service, there's no question about it, but it's very rewarding to have an impact, and I really think that is something that women should step up to the plate and do. I just hope we have more and more.

—KAY BAILEY HUTCHISON

Even though I think the political system is so corrupt and I believe in publicly financed elections and the media climate is terrible—all of these things—I still think there are women who totally have what it takes. They need to do it, and we need them to do it. And we need to support them in any way we can. I don't think we can wait until the political system feels more comfortable to those of us who don't have a high tolerance for that kind of stuff, because we will just be waiting forever. We've got to just jump in. Those of us who have that capacity, we really need them to take the risk and jump in, and the rest of us need to get behind them like crazy and make sure they feel supported.

—COURTNEY E. MARTIN

Even under the best of circumstances, politics is definitely a contact sport and you can get hurt in the process. But, to me, the reward of being able to implement policies that you know make life better for people outweighs the risks. And I think we need to teach young women to take risks, to understand that losing a race is not losing, really. It's just your next step on the way to winning.

—GLORIA FELDT

What women don't know enough is that when women run, they win as often as men do. In spite of the obstacles, when they do decide, "I'm going to do this because it's important," they do win as often.

—PAT MITCHELL

It's a wonderful time to be a female thinking about running for office, because there are so many opportunities, and you just have to be brazen and throw your hat in the ring and say, "Okay, I'm going to do this no matter what." You're going to get further than you think, and people are going to be way more understanding than you think. It's not a bad time at all to be a woman interested in political life. I think the sky's the limit.

—ILEANA ROS-LEHTINEN

What I would say is—and this is what Shirley Chisholm told me in '72—don't let this daunting task fool you and take you away from the real mission, [which] is you've got to not only play by their rules, but *change* their rules, because the rules of the game may not have been created for women or by women. And so when you get here, if you see something that's old school, that's part of the good old boys' network, don't go along to get along—get in here and try to change it. We've got to shatter these rules here in Congress. We've got to make the structural and systemic changes here, just as we have to do on the outside. And so, yes, it is daunting, but we can't let that overtake us.

—**BARBARA LEE**

At some point [public office] could dovetail or integrate with [women's] lives. That doesn't mean they have to necessarily start at a young age, like I did. I underscore that because I want them to at least understand that it doesn't necessarily mean they have to start at the beginning and devote their whole lives to it, but rather at some point when it works, to consider it as a potential option, a possibility, and not to ever remove it entirely from their list of options throughout life. Keep that option open for the future.

It may not work now, but it may work at some point in the future, and oftentimes women do raise their children and then decide to run for public office, and so many have. And there are others who are raising their young children and making it work alongside their public service.

So I encourage them to think about it and not think it's out of their realm, because it's very much within their realm. And the fact is there's a cause and effect between what happens and doesn't happen in their own lives—and that's true for women and true for society as a whole. It's a cause and effect, and if you get involved, you can make a difference and make your voice heard.

—OLYMPIA SNOWE

I think one of the major obstacles we face is that we keep thinking there's going to be a perfect moment, where someone is going to come to us and say, "Wow, you would be perfect to run for the United States Senate," or "I really think we should put you forward for state House or to become governor," and we think there's a perfect moment in which our children will be the right age, we'll have all the correct degrees, know the right people, we'll have had all the correct experiences—and that simply isn't how life works. And as women we're so caught up in doing everything right that I think we are sort of preconditioned to wait for the perfect time, and it just doesn't happen. And I still see that. Actually, I recently spoke to a bunch of young women in Washington, hundreds of young women who are politically active and in their twenties, and I said, "Look, the most important thing to learn is to just say 'yes.' Whenever the next opportunity comes to you, don't think about whether you have the right clothes, or you have the right degree, just say 'yes.'" And it was like dropping a match on kindling.

—CECILE RICHARDS

I just say to people, "Don't be intimidated by the fact that you're the first in your neighborhood to do whatever it is, to run for whatever office it is. Don't be intimidated by that. Somebody has to be first and it might as well be you."

—CAROL MOSELEY BRAUN

America needs you. Women, know your power, go for it, be yourself, don't be afraid, be confident, and be ready. The world is waiting for you.

—NANCY PELOSI

Q&A WITH KIRSTEN GILLIBRAND ON WHY WOMEN SHOULD CONSIDER RUNNING FOR OFFICE

We need women leading the way. I really think that until women are able to achieve their potential, America will not achieve hers.

—**Kirsten Gillibrand**

Kirsten Gillibrand is a New York senator. After first being elected to the House of Representatives in 2006, she was appointed to serve in the seat vacated by Hillary Clinton in January 2009. She won reelection in 2018 with 67 percent of the vote. In March 2019, she announced her run for president in 2020.

Gillibrand has made her presence felt in Washington as a leading voice for how to grow our economy, protect middle-class families, strengthen national security, end the war in Afghanistan, protect women's rights, and get women more engaged in the political process. Inspired by her grandmother, Kirsten has made it her life's mission to support and empower more women to step up and run for office. In 2010, Kirsten launched Off The Sidelines: a call to action to encourage women and girls to make their voices heard on the issues they care about. Off The Sidelines has recruited, mentored, and supported dozens of women candidates for higher office and helped elect some of the Democratic Party's brightest rising stars. Gillibrand is also the author of Off the Sidelines: Speak Up, Be Fearless, and Change Your World *and* Bold & Brave: Ten Heroes Who Won Women the Right to Vote, *a picture book that celebrates the courageous leaders of the women's suffrage movement.*

MARIANNE SCHNALL: Why do you feel it's so important for women to run for office?

KIRSTEN GILLIBRAND: I think women's views, values, and priorities are missing in the national and local debate, and I think if we heard more of them, it would make a difference. It's not just that I want women to run for office; I also want them to be active in their community, in every sphere, because their life experiences are really relevant to all levels of decision-making.

Our presence and power are growing, but it's not enough—Congress should be 51 percent female. Women bring a problem-solving approach to Washington, and Washington is broken, so it's very important to have women who are trying to reach across party lines and find common ground.

Women, we need you to be advocates, to be heard on the issues you care about, to be voting, to be running for office, to be part of decision-making. And on the economic side, if we are going to out-innovate, out-compete, and out-educate other countries, our competitors, we are only going to succeed if women are leading the way.

MS: What are the rewards of a career in elected office?

KG: You are serving the public for the greater good. It sometimes means you'll have less anonymity. You might have a different life than you would have otherwise if you were in the private sector, but overwhelmingly, it is so rewarding. If you know you're spending your life to help people, your job 24/7 is to make a difference in people's lives, it's so exciting and so rewarding.

I would encourage every woman, if they have any interests on any issue, that they should strive to serve on some level. Try to engage in public service. It's the only job I've ever had that I really feel like I can help people make a difference every day. And that's a huge gift; it's a wonderful opportunity.

I would encourage any young woman who is interested in starting out in public service or interning in a Senate office, that it's totally worth their time, because they'll find not only how rewarding it is to help others, but they'll find that their voice really is unique, that they have issues and passions that are not shared. And that, if they raise the things they care about, others will join them, and they can actually move a mountain.

MS: How do you think the recent influx of more women and diversity in Washington will affect the dynamics? What benefits do you think it will bring?

KG: You know, women's lives are very different. We have different life experiences, and our differences are our strength. We will bring knowledge of issues to the fore, we will raise different issues, we will offer different solutions, and I think these issues of right versus wrong are very much about why women ran. I think they believed generally that we should care about one another, that we should believe in the Golden Rule, that we should fight for other people's kids as hard as we fight for our own.

I think a lot of the women that ran and won have issues they want to be addressed and they are not going to give up, and that's what makes our country stronger. It's a revolutionary time because these women are not going to be part of the status quo and they are going to demand very different outcomes on issues that perhaps Congress ignores, like national paid leave or affordable daycare or equal pay.

MS: Politics is often described as gridlocked. Can you tell me about the bipartisan efforts that you and your female colleagues have demonstrated in the Senate?

KG: More often than not, women are quite collaborative in nature. More often than not, they not only listen well to each other, but they reach for common ground. They actually want to get things done. And they can leave their egos at the door. They can leave their political parties at the door and really move forward on real substantive ideas. I've seen that in my time in the Senate. I've seen women from both sides of the aisle come together, work together to get things done, because it's more important to them to actually accomplish something than score political points.

Every bill I've ever passed, I've had strong Republican women helping me. So I feel that Republican women, along with Democratic women, together will try very hard to get things done, more so than our male colleagues on any given day.

Those women in the Senate, and in other places as well, really do find the common ground and make Washington work in a very different way. So I really believe the presence of women at decision-making tables is overwhelmingly impactful and can make the difference between reaching the right result and reaching the wrong result.

MS: **How do you view where women stand today, with the surge of women running for office and the recent wins in the midterms, contrasted against the stark reality of the continued glaring inequity, as well as the current attacks that we face on women's rights and freedoms?**

KG: I think this moment that we are in was spurred by the desire to be heard in light of the country electing President Trump. The Women's March was the day after the inauguration. The fact that millions of people marched worldwide to be heard and the fact that those marchers were intersectional. The fact that it didn't matter if your sign said "Women's Reproductive Freedom" or "Black Lives Matter" or "Rights for Muslims" or "Immigrant Rights" or "LGBTQ Equality" or "Clean Air, Clean Water." It just mattered that you felt passionate that your voice wasn't being heard.

And that momentum that was created didn't stop—women continued to show up at town halls, continued to protest outside senators' and Congress members' offices, held vigils during the Kavanaugh hearings, and the fact that we had more women running than before in the history of the country, more women winning than ever before: the huge numbers of women of color who ran, having two Native American women running and winning, having Muslim women running and winning, having far more black women and Latinas running. It makes a difference. Now we are going to have a broader voice in Congress.

MS: Fundraising remains a substantial barrier for women who are running for office. In your experience, what is the biggest contributor to that obstacle? And how do we change it?

KG: For a lot of women, when they're first running for office, they feel that it's arrogant or conceited that they think they should be elected to something. I certainly felt that way. And what you learn in a campaign is that resources, and money specifically, are necessary to explain to people why you're running, what you care about, what you're going to do when you get there. And it's actually not about you. It's about the causes and issues that you care about and what problem you're going to solve and what group of people you're going to help.

As soon as you tell a female candidate that that's why she's raising money, that's why she's asking people for help, for the cause or the issue that she cares deeply about, it makes it so much easier. Because if she realizes when you're asking someone for $100, it's not for yourself, it's that you care about school lunch programs, or you care about hunger in America, or you care about global climate change, whatever it is that drives you, that's why you're asking for the money. As soon as a female candidate recognizes that, she can raise unlimited amounts of money, and it becomes much easier.

MS: Looking back, what piece of advice would have served you best at the beginning of your political career?

KG: To not be afraid. I was very intimidated about public service and about running for office, certainly throughout my twenties and early thirties. And so I got involved. I started working on other people's campaigns. I helped Hillary get elected to the Senate. I helped her husband in his presidential runs. I helped a lot of local candidates run for State Senate and State Assembly and City Council in New York City. The more I got involved, the more I realized I really enjoyed politics, and I really wanted, personally, to do public service. I just didn't quite have the courage.

And so, over about a ten-year period, through helping others, working on campaigns, I developed enough confidence to actually run for office myself. And it took time. If I could do it over, I would have tried to get there a little sooner. But you know, things happen for a reason, and throughout that ten years, I really learned a lot about organizing and creating grassroots support for things that I cared about, candidates I cared about.

MS: Where do you get your strength?

KG: I get my strength from my faith and from the people around me who are also fighting with me side by side. In the early days of the Kavanaugh hearings, I was beginning to say, "How are we ever going to defeat this nominee?" But I would just go to one of the rallies and I would see all these women carrying their signs, speaking out, wanting to be part of this debate, and I thought, *If they can fight one more day, I can fight one more day.*

MS: What advice do you have in terms of people finding their own pathway right now to make a difference?

KG: The most important message that I give to young kids and to people I meet across my state, across the country, is that their voices matter. This is a moment in time where we cannot stay silent, that we must speak up. . . . You have to fight back, you have to speak out. You have to do whatever your time and talents will allow you to do to make a difference.

And my advice to women is this: don't wait for some white knight in Washington to ride up and save us. You will wait forever. It is the grassroots who will create the message, launch the campaigns, and win the elections that finally change our country for the better.

9

THERE ARE MANY WAYS TO
BE A LEADER AND ENACT CHANGE

There are multiple levels of leadership. Your leadership in
your own family, your community, how you lead your life,
how you present yourself in the world as one who is willing
to use what you have to give to others. That to me is the
defining meaning of what it takes to be a leader.
—Oprah Winfrey

Despite the tumultuous and concerning times we have been living through in this country, something positive has emerged: a heightened and unprecedented level of civic engagement and activism. Not only are more women running for office, but they are also using their voices as advocates for change in all kinds of ways—marching in historic numbers, voting, sharing their stories, contacting their representatives, donating to and volunteering for causes they believe in. Women are advocating for change to address problems ranging from climate change to gun violence to sexual harassment, racism, immigrant rights, economic inequality, and a host of other serious issues facing our country.

All of our voices matter, and we each have something powerful and unique to offer—even speaking out against a sexist or racist comment is a form of leadership.

We can all be agents of change and experience the rewards of being a part of a hopeful, positive movement to create a better world.

Stay engaged at whatever level—it doesn't have to be elected office. There are many ways to be a leader.

—ARIANNA HUFFINGTON

Not everybody needs to run for office. Some people need to be better advocates in their neighborhood. Some people need to be better advocates when it comes to fixing up schools and keeping the community thriving. Some people need to be better advocates in terms of the environment. So there are many ways to serve and many ways that we can fulfill our role as citizens of the United States of America.

—DONNA BRAZILE

In every respect I want to encourage and support people in leadership positions. But I think it's important to remind everyone there are two paths. And you can argue that one is not necessarily superior to the other. [There is] formal authority—being president, being elected into a position of influence and power—but one can make a legitimate argument that that may not necessarily be the most influential place to be. There are two points of authority, and that's moral versus formal authority.

When you think about people like Václav Havel or Dr. Martin Luther King Jr. or Gandhi, people like Mandela, you can argue that at the peak of their influence when they had the most impact in the world and in their countries, they shared two things in common: one was jail time, and two was that none of them had formal authority at the peak of their influence. You can make a very good case that when Mandela became president for his one term and Václav Havel—he made this case when he was president, as well—that they lost a little bit of their authority, even though they became presidents of their respective countries, because their voices were so much more powerful when they were exercised autonomously from the formal connections within governing organizations, with all of those rules and regulations and all of the limitations and formal laws of governing.

So for me, leadership is not about being something in order to do something. And I think it's incredibly important for women to recognize that you don't need to be president, you don't need to be governor, you don't need to be mayor, you don't even need to be in elected office to be a leader and aspire to influence. I mean, what's the purpose of leadership? It's to move people to a cause greater than themselves and to have an impact that transcends. You can manifest that in so many different ways; you don't have to limit yourself to formal authority. So as important as it is to be a mayor, a governor, a president, whatever it may be, one could argue that it may not be the apex of leadership—that there are other ways to truly change the world that perhaps have even more meaning and impact. And so I just hope we encourage our young girls to aspire to that consideration and not just to the limited consideration of a formal role in society.

There are so many other ways to contribute and to lead and to change the world. You don't have to be in elected office, though it remains powerfully important and we need to encourage [it] more.

—GAVIN NEWSOM

FOUR KEYS TO BEING A CHANGEMAKER

1. START LOCALLY

You know the little saying, "Think globally, act locally"? No, act locally first, see that you make a difference, then you dare to think globally.

—JANE GOODALL

A study found that the autonomous feminist movements are the key to changing violence against women. This is a study that's been conducted over four decades in seventy countries, and it revealed that the mobilization of feminist movements is more important for change than the wealth of nations, left-wing political parties, or the number of women politicians.

I've always felt the best way to make change is to work with the grassroots and to focus locally where you are in your own community.... There's plenty to do everywhere. When people say they don't know how to direct their energy, I want to say, "Walk outside." People are suffering everywhere—people looking for work and needing health care, people desperate to talk and tell their story. The world changes from the ground up.

—EVE ENSLER

Activism, traditionally, is easier to do when it seems like something that doesn't affect you directly. That's why people get so outraged by the Taliban, but don't get so outraged by the conditions in Brownsville, New York. I mean, people are so much more willing to care when it's farther away, in part because it seems much more desperate, but in part because you don't have to assume responsibility if it's happening so far away. It's a problem they can just help to "solve" without having to take responsibility. And I think that you actually have more effect and impact if you look at your own life and your own community and you start to make change in very minute ways there—and that, collectively, can add up to something much bigger.

—AMY RICHARDS

Change is like a house: you can't build it from the top down, only from the bottom up. Whatever small change we make will be like a pebble in a pond. It will reverberate outward and it will also be fun. We're meant to be active and contribute to the world. What's the alternative? Just sitting there and wondering, "Oh, if I had just done this, maybe . . ." I've learned one thing: no matter how hard it is to do it, it's harder *not* to do it. Then you're stuck with wondering, "What if I had said . . . ? What if I had done . . . ?"

—GLORIA STEINEM

I don't think it matters who you are, where you come from, or where you want to make your impact. You can make your impact on your neighborhood block. You can make your impact on your local school board. You can make your impact on any issue that you think is important. But the promise is, because you think it's important, it *is* important. Women's views and their values are important, and as they communicate their views and values, they will change outcomes. And it could be as local as their block, or as important as a national debate. It's important to be a voice for the cause that you're fighting for. I think all of us can use our voices to be as powerful as they can be, on any issue that we think is important.

—KIRSTEN GILLIBRAND

2. REMEMBER THAT SMALL ACTIONS MAKE A BIG DIFFERENCE

If we all do what little we can, collectively we can make a difference. There are very many little things that we all can do. And even though we think that a particular action at an individual level may be very small, just imagine if it is repeated several million times.

—WANGARI MAATHAI

Gandhi was correct: you have to be the change you want to see in the world. And it changes with one person at a time.

—OPRAH WINFREY

If we all give up hope and do nothing, then indeed there is no hope. It will be helped by all of us taking action of some sort.

Cumulatively, our small decisions, choices, and actions make a very big difference.

—JANE GOODALL

There are so many things that you can do. Look in the mirror and think about this: you've been commissioned to figure out how you, one person, can make a difference. Take on the responsibility of giving it some thought. Think of one thing, ten things, a hundred things, whatever it is. And then get the information out there. What do you have that is your personal power?

—DR. SYLVIA EARLE

Whatever you care about, you can make a difference. You really can. Don't ever underestimate yourself. Do not underestimate the human spirit.

—BILLIE JEAN KING

People think that if they can't wave their magic wand and change the whole world for the better overnight, there's no point. I want people to understand that it's all of the work that all of us do in different areas [that] makes the world a better place. No one person, no one issue, is the key to changing everything. And if we all contribute in our own way, even a couple of hours a month of volunteering meaningfully, how awesome would the world be?

—JODY WILLIAMS

Every time we have moved the arc of the moral universe, that very long arc in our nation's history, it's been because of ordinary people who got involved and decided to do extraordinary things.

—VALERIE JARRETT

3. EXPERIENCE THE JOY OF GIVING BACK

I got excited about [the Worldwide Orphans Foundation] because I saw the good work up close. . . . Like any social cause, you just meet some people who are doing some things, and you realize, "Ah! These forty children are different than they were a year ago, and these 250 will be different if I do this fundraiser, and maybe by the year's end, 1,800 children will have this," and it suddenly becomes a real thing and not this giant idea that you wish could get better. It was nice to be reminded of the rest of the world.

I think there's nothing wrong with giving your time and energy and money for very selfish reasons. If it makes you feel good, great. Just being outside of yourself . . . just to have a human connection that means something—again, it's a selfish feeling—it makes you feel good. There's nothing wrong with that.

—AMY POEHLER

I see a lot of people really wanting to do positive things in the world. And I feel that it's like a new generation. . . . I think volunteering is the most fun thing—it can be really amazing and rewarding and meaningful. Sometimes I feel like it's more for me. I mean, I'm not really helping them anywhere near as much as they are helping me. It completely broadens my view of the world.

—NATALIE PORTMAN

Giving, loving, caring, empathy, and compassion, going beyond ourselves and stepping out of our comfort zones to help serve others—this is the only viable answer to the multitude of problems the world is facing.

—ARIANNA HUFFINGTON

If [people] choose to get involved, they will be blown away by how joyful it actually is and how much fun it really is, and if they put their brains and their energy and their money behind something, they really can contribute to changing the world. And I believe that not just for somebody who's wealthy, but for somebody who volunteers in their local community and gives their time, too. There are a lot of benefits to giving back, time or resources, in either case.

—MELINDA GATES

4. TAKE ACTION

Don't agonize—*organize.* Just get out there and make the difference.

—NANCY PELOSI

I never said, "Ooh, I want to be an activist." I just found that the more I spoke my truth, the more activist I became. I am constantly amazed at how courageous and radical speaking the truth is. The most activist thing you can do is just speak the truth and search for the truth and just follow that trail, and it will come to you. Believe me, the universe will hand it to you.

—MELISSA ETHERIDGE

I think that now more than ever there are so many ways to get involved, especially if you're talking about politics or trying to change things. There are so many ways to just have a voice—to blog about things, to talk about things. People now have so much more access to information and spreading information. So this is the best time I can imagine ever to have a cause that you believe in and to really talk about it and to spread your message. It's amazing the power that everybody has to have a voice now. So to take that into consideration—that everybody who has access to a computer has the same power of voice [as] anybody else—it's really incredible.

—MARGARET CHO

If you want to be successful, if you want to experience real, true happiness and a true sense of reward, you'll find that in trying to be of service to others. If you see a problem, be a part of the solution. Don't stay on the sidelines and complain—take action.

—TULSI GABBARD

Our role is to dream a better world and to work courageously to make that dream possible.

—ISABEL ALLENDE

Take the tools and the skills and the resources of every kind that you have and go out, find something that you know is not fair, is not just, and begin to change it. In whatever way you know, in whatever way is appropriate for you, but don't ignore it. Don't think it's somebody else's job to change it. Confront it in your own way, and make it your job to make change.

—ANITA HILL

Q&A WITH GLORIA STEINEM ON CREATING POSITIVE CHANGE IN THE WORLD

Progress is not automatic—that's what movements are for. It depends on what we do every day.
—Gloria Steinem

Gloria Steinem is a renowned writer, speaker, and feminist activist. She travels in the United States and other countries as an organizer and lecturer and is a frequent media spokeswoman on issues of equality. In 1972 she cofounded Ms. *magazine, which has become a landmark in both women's rights and American journalism. She also cofounded Equity Now, Donor Direct Action, the National Women's Political Caucus, and the Women's Media Center, an organization that works to raise the visibility and decision-making power of women and girls in the media. Her books include the bestsellers* My Life on the Road, Revolution from Within, Outrageous Acts and Everyday Rebellions, *and* Moving Beyond Words. *She serves on the boards of the Women's Media Center, Equity Now, Donor Direct Action, and on the advisory board of Apne Aap. She is an advisor to TIME'S UP, part of a global movement against sexual harassment and violence. In 2013, President Obama awarded her the Presidential Medal of Freedom, the highest civilian honor.*

MARIANNE SCHNALL: How do you feel overall about where we are today in the arc of progress for women? Is significant progress still being made?

GLORIA STEINEM: I think we've just begun. We've accomplished some very important tasks. First, we know we're not crazy. The *system* is crazy. And this is very important. Second, we've built a majority support in this country and women's movements in many other countries, so instead of being a novelty, we are now a majority. And we have achieved new laws, new phrases, new definitions, new consciousness in very important and life-saving ways.

However, there is still so much violence against females in the world, whether it is son surplus and daughter deficit in Asia, or sexualized violence in war zones, or domestic violence here, or child marriage in many other countries. So violence against women is clearly not solved, not at all solved, and the reasons for it, which are controlling women's bodies in order to control reproduction, are definitely not solved.

MS: Do you think the notion of what feminism is today has changed since you began in the movement all those years ago?

GS: Yes and no. I think it has changed because we now better understand the links between equality for women and every other issue. For instance, now we understand that equal pay would be the best economic stimulus this country could have. We understand that violence against women is the biggest normalizer of all other violence, because it tends to be what people see first in their families or neighborhoods and it normalizes the idea that one group is born to dominate another. So I think we understand the connections much better. Not well enough, incidentally, because if we did, we would be screening our police for domestic violence, which is the biggest indicator of other violence and is a supremacy crime; both supremacy by sex and race is a parallel motivation. It's not getting you more money necessarily or benefiting you in any real way. It's just a question of having a superior identity. If we did something about the fact that cops have four times the rate of domestic violence that exists in the population at large, we would be screening out racist and sexist cops.

So we do understand the connections better, but I think the fundamental principles were clear—the first big issue was legalizing and making abortions safe, so we were understanding that women's existence as the means for reproduction was the fundamental reason for our inferior status; the desire to control reproduction was the fundamental reason.

MS: What will it take to address all of the issues and problems that have been plaguing our country and the world for so many years? Do you feel like there's anything we can do to speed progress up?

GS: Progress is not automatic—that's what movements are for. It depends on what we do every day. Change does come from the bottom up, and it will come from girls and women and men who understand that for us all to be human beings, instead of being grouped by gender, is good for them, too.

MS: There's been a lot of conversation not just about getting women in leadership but about what types of paradigms of leadership and power we most need now. Do you think that part of it is redefining how power is used?

GS: Yes, and that's been true from the beginning. In the late '60s, people were saying we need power to, not power over. Power to do, accomplish, create, not power over other people.

MS: What do you see as some of the challenges that women running for president face?

GS: There's going to be a demand for perfectionism on the part of any pro-equality woman candidate that would not be made of men. There are going to be attacks based on different standards of morality and different standards of dress and physical attractiveness. There are going to be men in the media, and perhaps some women, too, who perhaps unconsciously associate female authority with childhood, because that's the last time they saw a powerful woman, and so they feel threatened and regressed to childhood by the sight of a powerful woman outside of the home.

MS: What do you think it would actually mean for women and politics in our culture to have a woman president?

GS: It's important because, for one thing, little girls would look at themselves and women in a different way if they could imagine being the head of the country. It would free their hopes, and it would free the imaginations of little boys to see male *and* female authority. However, it doesn't necessarily change the structural problems just to have one person at the top.

And it's not just [about electing] a biological woman—it's a woman who stands for the majority issues and needs of women. It's not just getting a job for one woman, it's making life better for *all* women.

MS: Why is it so important for women to vote in every election?

GS: The voting booth is still the only place that a pauper equals a billionaire, and any woman equals any man. If we organized well from the bottom up—and didn't fall for the idea that our vote doesn't count; an idea nurtured by those who don't want us to use it—we could elect feminists, women of all races, and some diverse men, too, who actually represent the female half of the country equally. It's up to us.

If you don't stand up for yourself politically, no one else will. So we have to use our votes and our dollars and our voices to be engaged and involved in these issues. In every other arena we know that if we're not involved in a decision, it won't reflect our wishes. But many of us here have been conned into ceding our powers in the political arena. One vote does in fact count.

MS: How do you view the importance of women as truth tellers—of women speaking our truths right now, whether in the media or generally in all fields and in the wake of the #MeToo movement?

GS: It's always important that women tell the truth ourselves, and support other truth tellers. Everybody who led to this critical mass is important, and so are those who now use it to transform "masculine" and "feminine" roles into ways we can all be unique and equally valuable.

MS: What is your life philosophy?

GS: Some people live in the past, some people live in the present, which is probably the most rewarding, and some people live in the future. I live in the future, so I am always thinking, "What if?" or "This could be" or "This could change" or trying to understand why something happens. The great joy to me is that moment, that "Aha!," that excitement and pleasure in realizing why something is happening and how it could be different. That definitely keeps me going.

MS: Gloria, you're still writing and speaking and traveling. What personally drives you after all these years? What is the source of your energy that keeps you going?

GS: You and everybody we know who shares the same hopes. Excitement, because it's endlessly interesting to be organizing and hearing possible solutions or thinking of possible solutions and how to put efforts together. It makes everything else boring, actually.

MS: We talk a lot about all the challenges we face and all that's wrong in the world, but what right now gives you hope?

GS: Well, because I've just been traveling much more than usual, I've had an intense dose of just listening to the general public, so I got an explosion of consciousness. It comes out of both anger and despair and hope and accomplishment, but it's there. It's consciousness. It's incredible. I'm quite stunned by it. The consciousness is incredibly high because of Black Lives Matter and the cops and anger about election financing and global warming—and none of these problems can be solved without the female half of the population, and obviously seeing it that way creates new solutions.

MS: I detect that, too. The shift that's happening.

GS: It's interesting because I don't exactly know how to explain it. It is partly the Web because people can discover supportive information out of time, so people who are sixteen who might not otherwise know about me or you, know about me and you. I think there's more ability to realize there are shared concerns and shared values without the traditional media.

MS: Exactly. So there's more access to information and ways to use our voices.

GS: And at the same time, people want to be together, physically. There is a longing, as we see in our communal lives, to be in a group, to sit around a campfire, to talk to each other, to tell our stories and listen to other people's stories.

MS: It's so easy to feel frustrated and powerless with all that's happening in the world today. What advice would you give to

people who feel disillusioned or cynical or powerless about what they can do?

GS: The forces they want to rebel against have put a lot of effort into making them feel powerless. But the fact is that every single issue we care about is now a majority issue. In most cases where we have lost or are losing, it's because we haven't paid attention. For instance, state legislatures. Most Americans don't know who their state legislators are, so most state legislators are run by the interests they regulate. It's up to us to know who our state legislators are and pay attention, at least as much attention in states as we do in Washington.

MS: What message do you think is important for people to internalize today, in terms of how they can be a part of creating positive change?

GS: I would say don't worry about what you *should* do; do whatever you can. And seek companions with shared values. If we're isolated, we come to feel powerless when we're not.

10

PUT YOURSELF FIRST

I try to put myself first. If I don't put my own physical and emotional health first, then I'm not really useful to any movement, to any work of art, to any creative endeavor. I have to be aware—not selfish and self-absorbed and self-obsessed—but I have to be self-aware of what my needs are and be willing to take care of my own needs.

—Kerry Washington

These days, one of the hardest and yet most important priorities for women is taking care of ourselves. As a busy woman myself, who is juggling myriad work and family responsibilities, and a seemingly never-ending to-do list, I can attest to how challenging this is—especially when things like social media, the onslaught of the news cycle, and frequent lack of sleep are near-constant distractions and impediments to our self-care.

But as women, we must continue to be intentional about prioritizing our needs, our well-being, and some unplugged alone time. If we don't, then everything suffers: our productivity, our health, our ability to be present for our friends and families, and our overall quality of life.

For me (and for many others I have interviewed, like Jane Fonda, Goldie Hawn, and Oprah Winfrey), meditation is an example of one of the practices I try to do daily to nourish and center myself. What is it for you? Perhaps you will find some inspiration and ideas in the words that follow.

FIVE KEYS TO PUTTING YOURSELF FIRST

---

1. LEARN TO SAY NO

In our society, there's a belief that a good, nurturing woman gives and gives and gives until she drops. If she takes time for herself, she is selfish. Too many of us buy into this belief and give and give and give until we're so exhausted we can hardly move. And then we give some more!

I've dealt with this. For a while, especially after my first book was published, I was asked to emcee events, sit on boards, and write essays and endorsements for various groups and papers. As I said yes to these requests, there was a small voice in me that kept saying, "Soon people will realize I'm exhausted and stop asking. Someone please speak up for me so I don't have to say no."

The first thing I had to learn was to speak up for myself. I learned to say no. Then I learned to choose and pick groups whose missions match my heart and passion.

—LOUNG UNG

2. TAKE TIME FOR YOU

It is amazing how even ten minutes without your cell phone or computer or TV—just you and silence—can wake you up and fill your empty well. Just shutting the door and telling everybody,

"Don't bother me for ten little minutes." That's your sacred time to either sit nice and tall, breathe or stretch, or do some physical exercise that awakens the energy inside of you. Even ten minutes a day is really helpful, and I absolutely do not believe that anyone doesn't have ten minutes a day. But it takes some degree of discipline. This is why most spiritual paths are called a discipline or a practice. A practice is something that you have to make yourself do, but the result is becoming better at the art of living.

—ELIZABETH LESSER

The most important relationship in life is the one you have with yourself. That's number one.

—DIANE VON FURSTENBERG

I schedule things. I schedule time with friends, I schedule time to meditate, and I schedule time to do some kind of working out, even if that just means walking. "Discipline is liberation"—that's Martha Graham. So when you're disciplined, then you can make sure that the things that are important to your psyche, to your life, to your well-being actually happen. It liberates you.

—JANE FONDA

My encouragement to all women is, Let us try to offer help before we have to offer therapy. Let's see if we can't prevent being ill by trying to offer a love of prevention before illness, so that we don't have to wait to get sick and then try to find a way to heal ourselves. Let's do the right thing—that is, really be on our own side. I think that's the wisest thing: to prevent illness before we try to cure something.

—MAYA ANGELOU

I think what you do is you learn to relax . . . because that's when you have time to read, you have time to reflect, you have time to nourish. If you are careful, if you plan your work, you do find time to nourish yourself.

—WANGARI MAATHAI

3. FIND HAPPINESS WITHIN

To paraphrase Camus, even in the midst of winter, I find within me an invincible summer. I am a big believer that the unexamined life is not worth living. The first place to go is within and really examine what your own process is and all the pieces of you. Then you will find within you what you desperately want. You will find the strength that is just there. There is your invincible summer. It isn't always outside you. It isn't always somebody else that's going to help you feel seen and teach you the strength of your voice. In most instances, it's going to come from within.

—SALLY FIELD

Happiness has to come from feeling a sense of well-being within yourself. If it doesn't, then you're grasping outside for all the things that you think are going to make you happy—whether it's a job or money or status or recognition—all of these aspects of ego that are being fed. To me it's that incredible sense of belonging and peace within your own self and heart that really is joy. You own it. It is all yours, nobody else's.

—GOLDIE HAWN

4. PRACTICE STILLNESS OR MEDITATION

One practice I rely on all the time is basic meditation, which allows me to strip away the noise. It's like the old-fashioned dial on the radio, where you were getting static and then you found that clear, sweet spot on the dial where the music would come through. That's what meditation is for me. Dialing out the static, the noise, the anxiety, the fear, and coming into a place that's deep and quiet. It's like dropping into a well of inspiration and wisdom.

I recommend learning how to come into the presence of stillness and vastness. Learn any form of meditation. Spend twenty minutes every day if possible in meditation, listening to the crazy monkey mind inside you and learning how to still the thoughts and discover that big, deep, soulful part of yourself. If you do that, it actually becomes something that you can call up at will in a hard meeting, on a crowded subway, in a difficult conversation—you can return to that still, wise voice within.

—ELIZABETH LESSER

I think that silence is the best way to get real attention, especially from the deep self. In my own case, I know that what I can bring to the world comes from a world of deep silence and quiet. That is where my compass—my moral compass and my internal guide—that's where they live, in that deep quiet.

We do carry an inner light, an inner compass, and the reason we don't know we carry it is because we've been distracted. We think that the light is actually being carried by a leader or somebody that we have elected or somebody that we very much admire, and that that's the only light. We forget that we have our own light—it may be small, it may be flickering, but it's actually there. So what we need to do is to be still enough to let that light shine and illuminate our inner landscape and our dreams—especially our dreams. And then our dreams will lead us to the right way.

—ALICE WALKER

You know what happens if you're completely still? Your mind—that little tape that's running *bup, bup, bup*, all the noise—it eventually runs off the reel. And you have nothing left to think. All of a sudden, the answers are just there.

—MELISSA ETHERIDGE

The way to get back to yourself is to literally get still and be alone and to drown out the voices of the world so that you can find your own way, because your own way is always right here. Glinda the Good Witch is really one of my greatest spiritual teachers, because

Glinda says to Dorothy, "You always had it." That really is the way. You can spend all the years of your life looking outside of yourself for the answers to "Why am I here?" and "What am I really supposed to do?" but only when you are conscious enough to connect to the stillness can you really find the answers.

It always comes back to stillness. Open your heart, get still, ask the question for yourself, and the answer will reveal itself. There's no question you can ask for which there isn't an answer.

Let me just tell you, I don't know how you survive in today's world with all of the noise and the literal craziness that we are surrounded and bombarded with from the time you wake up in the morning—it's coming through on the radio, it's on your smartphones—from the moment you turn on any electronic anything, you are bombarded by negative noise. If you have not prepared yourself, you then become a receptacle for all of that energy. So I literally prepare myself to be shielded from all of the negativity. If you don't do that, then you will take on all the negative energy that is around you. And that's why by the end of the day, you feel crazy, too! When I don't prepare myself, I feel by midday stress and negativity and a depletion of energy.

If I have the time, it's twenty minutes of silence, or sometimes it's not. Now I have on my little timer: twelve. I've narrowed it down to twelve because most days I don't have time for twenty. But even if I don't have twelve, I take time just in the shower, while I'm letting the conditioner go through my hair, just to be still and fully present to order intentionally what I want for the day.

—OPRAH WINFREY

The sacred sauce, I think, is quieting the mind three times a day. Besides quieting down your emotional brain, this is actually focusing on your attention level and on your well-being. It strengthens your brain, so it's vitally important. And the research on [quieting the mind for] twenty minutes a day shows that actually a more frequent, shorter period is just as valuable, if not more. Which means if you spend three minutes in the morning, and then you go to lunch and do another three minutes, and then before you get into your house you do another three minutes, and then before you go to sleep, you can lie on your bed and do another three minutes—it's that kind of habituated training that the brain loves. And that's exactly what starts you shifting your way of thinking and your way of feeling.

—GOLDIE HAWN

We must be willing to challenge the assumption that time spent in relaxation and meditation takes away from our realizing other goals, such as a successful career or successful relationships. As paradoxical as it may seem, when we take time for meditation we actually gain in the other areas of our lives. The truth is, there's no limit to the positive changes we can make for ourselves and for our society through mindfulness meditation.

—THICH NHAT HANH

5. CONNECT WITH NATURE

I'm in awe of nature; not only is it beautiful, it's perfection. [Connecting with nature] is really important. Unfortunately, we don't get to do it very often in the nature that is truly nature. But go to the park; I love going to the park. Whenever I'm in a city, I always go to the gardens, and I'll just take off my shoes and put my foot right on the ground. And I like hugging trees, too. It does connect you in a totally different way.

—CAMERON DIAZ

I'm very lucky that I live in nature. I feel really blessed that I get to be in the wildness of nature because it reminds me of the wild parts of my mind and heart.

—ELIZABETH LESSER

What touches me is a great spiritual power. . . . I felt it especially out in the forest, out in nature, being part of the whole—the amazing extraordinary universe.

—JANE GOODALL

Have you ever gone out and looked at the stars? I actually walked up the mountain in back of my house in Maui and camped out in the night at the top. And I advise everybody to do that, even if you go to your backyard at some point. Looking up at the stars and realizing that you are made of the star stuff—that this is where you come from and no matter what you know, you don't know it all.

—OPRAH WINFREY

Q&A WITH ARIANNA HUFFINGTON ON HOW TO PRACTICE SELF-CARE

We've devalued relaxation and downtime to the point of stigmatizing them.
—Arianna Huffington

Arianna Huffington founded and is the former president and editor in chief of The Huffington Post, *a Pulitzer Prize–winning news and blog site that is one of the most widely read, linked to, and frequently cited media brands on the Internet.*

In 2007, after collapsing from sleep deprivation and exhaustion, she "became more and more passionate about the connection between well-being and performance" and made it her mission to end the stress and burnout epidemic. She is the founder and CEO of Thrive Global, an organization that helps individuals, companies, and communities improve their well-being and performance and unlock their greatest potential. She is the author of fifteen books, including Thrive: The Third Metric to Redefining Success and Creating a Life of Well-Being, Wisdom, and Wonder *and* The Sleep Revolution: Transforming Your Life, One Night at a Time.

She has been named to Time *magazine's list of the world's 100 most influential people and* Forbes' *World's 100 Most Powerful Women list. She serves on numerous boards, including the Center for Public Integrity and the Committee to Protect Journalists.*

MARIANNE SCHNALL: What advice do you have for women who are often struggling to balance it all and don't prioritize their own self-care?

ARIANNA HUFFINGTON: The better people are at taking care of themselves, the more effective they'll be in taking care of others, including their families, coworkers, communities, and fellow citizens. When you're on an airplane, you're told to "secure your own mask first before helping others," even your own child. After all, it's not easy to help somebody else breathe easier if you're fighting for air yourself.

MS: What personal practices do you integrate into your own very busy life?

AH: I have worked to integrate certain practices into my day—meditation, walking, exercise—but the connection that conscious breathing gives me is something I can return to hundreds of times during the day in an instant. A conscious focus on breathing helps me introduce pauses into my daily life, brings me back into the moment, and helps me transcend upsets and setbacks. It has also helped me become much more aware when I hold or constrict my breath, not just when dealing with a problem, but sometimes even when I'm doing something as mundane as putting a key in the door, texting, reading an email, or going over my schedule. When I use my breath to relax the contracted core of my body, I can follow this thread back to my center. And, of course, getting enough sleep.

MS: For many people, the reason they have problems falling asleep at night has to do with an inability to turn our minds off. How much do you think that is linked with all the over-stimulation of our day, which has been exacerbated by all our busyness and constant inputs through technology?

AH: There's a direct link. Technology has allowed a growing number of us to carry our work with us—in our pockets and purses in the form of our phones—wherever we go. Our houses, our bedrooms, even our beds are littered with beeping, vibrating, flashing screens. It's the never-ending possibility of connecting—with friends, with strangers, with the entire world, with every TV show or movie ever made—with just the press of a button that is, not surprisingly, addictive. Humans are social creatures; we're hardwired to connect. Even when we're not actually connecting digitally, we're in a constant state of heightened anticipation. And always being in this state doesn't exactly put us in the right frame of mind to wind down when it's time to sleep.

We can manage our collective addiction by unplugging and recharging in various ways: meditation, long walks, exercise, yoga, reconnecting with family and/or friends. All this will increase some aspect of our well-being and sense of fulfillment.

Another thing keeping us up is worrying about our never-completed to-do lists. We lie in bed thinking of all that was not done today and all that needs to be done tomorrow, and it seems impossible to shut our minds off. I have a quote by Ralph Waldo Emerson by my bed that helps me silence my mind: "Finish every day, and be done with it. You have done what you could. Some blunders and absurdities no doubt crept in. Forget them as fast as you can.

Tomorrow is a new day. You shall begin it well and serenely, and with too high a spirit to be encumbered with your old nonsense."

MS: Do you think people have forgotten how to relax, or even know what to do with downtime?

AH: On a collective level, we've devalued relaxation and downtime to the point of stigmatizing them. And so much of our society is still operating under the collective delusion that sleep is simply time lost to other pursuits, that it can be endlessly appropriated at will to satisfy our increasingly busy lives and overstuffed to-do lists. We see this delusion reflected in the phrase "I'll sleep when I'm dead," which has flooded popular consciousness. Everywhere you turn, sleep deprivation is glamorized and celebrated: "You snooze, you lose." The phrase "catch a few z's" is telling: the last letter of the alphabet used to represent that last thing on our culture's shared priority list.

For me, going from sleep amateur to sleep pro meant trying a lot of things and seeing what worked. Here are some of the things I've tried. If any of these resonate with you, give them a try, too—keep what works, and discard the rest. It doesn't matter how hokey or unsophisticated a particular technique might feel; all that matters is did it help you get a good night's sleep?

One image I like to use is that of a calm lake. Any thought, worry, or concern that comes up, I think of as a stone dropping into the lake. There may be a ripple or two, but quickly the lake returns to its smoothness and calm. As more thoughts or worries or fears come up, I let them drop like stones and let the lake return to its natural tranquility.

Another technique that works for me is conscious breathing—using my breath to slow myself down and relax any tense areas in my body. As our breath flows in and out, our tensions gradually give way, as if our breath is massaging us from the inside out, releasing the stresses of the day we're still needlessly holding on to. As we get ready for sleep, we can practice seeing ourselves not as a closed, contracted fist but as supple and relaxed as a sleeping baby.

MS: How would you describe the benefits of meditation?

AH: What study after study shows is that meditation and mindfulness training profoundly affect every aspect of our lives—our bodies, minds, physical health, and our emotional and spiritual well-being. It's not quite the fountain of youth, but it's pretty close. When you consider all the benefits of meditation—and more are being found every day—it's not an exaggeration to call meditation a miracle drug.

MS: What advice do you have on getting started with meditation?

AH: Here are some simple steps to get you started meditating:

- Choose a reasonably quiet place to begin your practice, and select a time when you will not be interrupted.

- Relax your body. If you would like to close your eyes, do so. Allow yourself to take deep, comfortable breaths, gently noticing the rhythm of your inhalation and exhalation.

- Let your breathing be full—bring your attention to the air coming in your nostrils, filling up your abdomen, and then releasing. Gently and without effort, observe your breath flowing in and out.

- When thoughts come in, simply observe them and gently nudge your attention back to the breath. Meditation is not about stopping thoughts, but recognizing that we are more than our thoughts and our feelings. You can imagine the thoughts as clouds passing through the sky. If you find yourself judging your thoughts or feelings, simply bring yourself back to the awareness of the breath.

- Some people find it helpful to have a special or sacred word or phrase that they use to bring their awareness back to the breath. Examples include "om," "hu," "peace," "thank you," "grace," "love," and "calm." You can think of that word each time you inhale, or use it as your reminder word if your mind starts to wander.

- It is really important not to make your meditation practice one more thing you stress about. In fact, reducing stress is one of the major benefits of meditation together with increased intuition, creativity, compassion, and peace.

11

CREATE A HEALTHY WORK-LIFE BALANCE

I think the dialogue on whether or not women can have it all is incredibly harmful. We need to recognize that we can't do it all, that we face trade-offs every single minute of the day. We have to stop beating ourselves up for not doing everything perfectly.
—Sheryl Sandberg

One of the impediments that holds women back from advancing in their careers and into leadership positions is the very real challenge women face in balancing work and family. Culturally, women are still expected to be the primary caretakers of the home and children (and increasingly of elderly parents as well), and when we also want to have fulfilling careers, follow our passions, and be leaders, the load of those responsibilities can make it especially challenging to achieve all that we want to achieve (much less find the time to take care of ourselves! See the previous chapter).

Some of the solutions to this problem may come in the form of workplace policies that support working mothers and families, such as family leave, better childcare options, affordable daycare, pay equity, and flexible scheduling. The other aspect of addressing this problem comes in helping men break out of their stereotypical roles, so that they, too, can share in the responsibilities of taking care of the home and family. We need to redefine gender roles and raise boys to understand that these qualities are not "unmanly." After all, many men today are increasingly expressing a desire to work less and have more time to spend with their children and families, so these types of changes would benefit us all. In fact, research and case studies have found that when companies offer family-friendly policies and programs that allow for their employees to have more time with their families, the employees are more engaged, loyal, and productive. Plus, it improves the company's bottom line.

We also have to dismiss the damaging idea that women should be able to "do it all" or "have it all." Many women define their worth as being tied to being on top of home and work responsibilities at all times and being able to perfectly manage all of those responsibilities without anything falling through the cracks. That is an impossible bar to reach for, and one women need to let go of! Women need to ask for and receive the support we need—from our employers, from our partners, from our family members—in order to better balance work and home, set more realistic expectations for ourselves, advance in our careers, and achieve our goals.

The discussion about finding balance and raising your family and putting food on the table at the same time is a universal challenge, and if we're not supporting women in the workplace, then we're not doing our jobs. So I think if all of us could, on some level, rise up and be heard on why creating a better workplace for all parents and all working women is so important, we'll have a stronger economy and a stronger workforce. Things will be better on so many different levels.

Mothers often want to enter the workforce, but don't have the childcare or the support they need to do so. So [we need to] make sure employers know that when they provide childcare services, or when they make it easier for parents to work, they are increasing access to very good workers and to who's available for the workforce. It's a very pro-economy issue if you can provide affordable daycare. A lot of studies show that if you do that, if you provide it on-site or make it accessible, [then] actually a lot of parents are more productive workers as a result. So there is a lot of upside to it.

I think the most important message for women is that they can do it . . . that you can find a way to balance a career and family, that there is a way that you can be part of the decision-making fabric of this country and still be a good mother.

—KIRSTEN GILLIBRAND

Women have had more opportunities to go into different fields of work, but caring for families—that first piece of work, in the home—was never given its due value and recognition. That leaves us in the same cycle working-class and poor women have always been in. Women are doing two and three times the amount of work than is humanly possible.

There's still a tremendous amount that we have to do to bring recognition to that work, to figure out how we account for it, how we value it, and how we protect it. It begins with domestic workers still being excluded from some of the most basic labor laws, which is an indication of the kind of shifts that need to happen for us to have a truly sustainable economy in an environment that works for women. If you were to bring value and respect to that work, it would be a much more equitable distribution of work all around and a much better work-family balance for everyone, not just for women.

Today women are more than half of the workforce, do a vast majority of the caregiving work, represent more than half of the electorate, and live longer. Women are a driving force in society and the economy, so it's essential that we finish that unfinished business.

—AI-JEN POO

Men need to do more childcare and housework. We need to get to equality in the home. We cannot have equality in the office until we have equality in the home. It can't happen.

I think equal maternity and paternity leave are hugely important. How are we going to teach men to be equals if the average woman takes three months and the average man takes two weeks? People forget that there's a huge gap in our coverage.

—SHERYL SANDBERG

Men who see their enlightened self-interests in getting rid of gender categories and race categories are allies in a very reliable way because they see it as beneficial to themselves, as well as females as a group. [These are] men who really want to have a relationship with their children and raise their kids and have job patterns that allow them to do that—men who don't want to die early of violence and tension-related causes understand that this cause is mutual.

For a man to say, "I have to leave work now because I need to do something with my kids," it's sometimes viewed as a career killer. He doesn't have the right drive. So when they depart from their gender roles, they face some of the same restrictions. And more and more men are raising children or want to be close to their kids. They don't want to just lead work-obsessed lives and end up fifty years later with an engraved watch.

[To make it work, we need to] raise our sons more like our daughters, which means raising sons with the qualities you need to raise children, whether or not those sons have children. They're all qualities wrongly called feminine: attention to detail, patience, empathy. I don't have children, but I was raised as a female to have those qualities because they're perceived as feminine. Until men are raised with those qualities, too, they won't have the full circle of human qualities. Women tend to become whole people by venturing outside of the home, learning to aspire, to achieve, to deal with conflict—all these qualities that are wrongly called masculine. Men tend to gain wholeness by acquiring the qualities that are wrongly called feminine.

The deepest change begins with men raising children as much as women do and women being equal actors in the world outside the home. There are many ways of supporting that, from something as simple as paid sick leave and flexible work hours to attributing an economic value to all caregiving, and making that amount tax deductible.

Unless men are as responsible for babies and little children as women are, it will never work. I think it's terribly important that we always assume that men have, or should have, or could have, the same concerns about their kids that women do. Otherwise, a family-friendly policy will be seen as a penalty of employing women. More important, kids will grow up without nurturing fathers, and then they will remanufacture the masculine roles, both gender roles, because that's what they've seen in their household. So nothing could be more important than assuming that men need to be asking how can they combine work and family just as much as women do. Men need these child-friendly, family-friendly policies just as much as women do.

—GLORIA STEINEM

This whole juggling work and family, sure, it's reality. It's a difficult endeavor day-to-day. We live in a busy world, and trying to meet that demand and making sure your children are taken care of is difficult. And is there adequate childcare? I worked a lot on that issue over the years: affordable, accessible, quality childcare. That makes a profound difference in the working lives of women and, yes, men.

—OLYMPIA SNOWE

Women are still the primary people expected to raise the children and take care of the home; women are still expected to deal with that balancing act, and without much help from the workplace or the business they work for. And that is, by the way, where the necessity for having women leaders rests. Because I don't believe that we're going to change that set of challenges until women look at it and go, "My business can do this, my company can do that, my government can do this," whether your government is a city or whatever, and start to demand it.

—PAT MITCHELL

It always surprises me, the hunger women have. You can almost hear a collective sigh and see collective shoulders dropping down from ears and a relaxation when you say things like, "Do you think your workweek is way too long and each day extends too long, so that this battle you're in every day is, How do I balance children and home with work?" It shocks me that these conversations aren't happening more, but it also touches me that there's a great hunger for something other than just power for power's sake, money for money's sake. Women seem right away to light up and say, "Oh my God, we've got to talk about this. This isn't being talked about. What do we want to create with our power?"

Also, [there's] this kind of looking around guiltily, like, "Am I allowed to talk about this? Is there really room in any conversation about leadership to talk about my health, my depression, my fears, my children, my marriage? Is there room in this conversation? Isn't that getting too personal? Isn't that mixing work and home life?" And with the tiniest bit of encouragement—like, "No, it's appropriate; it's valid."

We've got to lead in this area. We've got to talk about child-care, maternity and paternity leave, shared jobs, priorities for governments. We've got to talk about this. We can't only talk about equal pay and gender parity in heads of corporations. We've got to talk about the why—there's a hunger in women if you get them alone in a room and give them props.

—ELIZABETH LESSER

Q&A WITH TIFFANY DUFU ON WHY IT'S OKAY FOR WOMEN TO "DROP THE BALL"

Now, more than ever, I just don't feel like we have the luxury of not being leaders. I would love for us to have more women whose bandwidth is freed up, especially psychologically, but also just literally, so that they can aspire to the highest level.

—Tiffany Dufu

Tiffany Dufu is a catalyst-at-large in the world of women's leadership and the author of Drop the Ball: Achieving More by Doing Less, *a memoir and manifesto that shows women how to cultivate the single skill they really need in order to thrive: the ability to let go.*

Tiffany is the founder and CEO of The Cru, a peer coaching platform for women looking to accelerate their professional and personal growth. She was a launch team member for Lean In and was chief leadership officer at Levo, one of the fastest-growing millennial professional networks. Prior to that, Tiffany served as president of The White House Project, as a major gifts officer at Simmons University in Boston, and as associate director of development at Seattle Girls' School. She was named to Fast Company's League of Extraordinary Women. *Tiffany serves on the boards of Girls Who Code and Simmons University.*

MARIANNE SCHNALL: You wrote a book called *Drop the Ball*, which is essentially about women realizing that they don't have to do it all and that it's okay to "drop the ball" in order to focus on the most important things in life, including taking on leadership roles. How did your drop-the-ball journey begin?

TIFFANY DUFU: I have spent the vast majority of my career on collective solutions to women's leadership challenges, which is that we don't have enough [women] at the highest level. And I kept having this experience where I would get up for forty-five minutes to an hour, [and] I would talk about our collective solutions to the women's leadership challenge. I would talk about equal pay for work. I would talk about workplace flexibility and affordable childcare and all of the public policies and corporate practices that I thought were really important [and] that we needed in order to create environments where women could bring their full self to the table. And one of the things that would happen is right after I would finish talking, the first set of questions that I would get during the Q&A were always personal questions that, to me, had nothing to do with what I had spoken about. A woman would raise her hand and she would say, "I noticed during your talk you said something about your daughter who's five and something about your son who's eight and your husband, he's in Dubai right now, and you're in San Francisco with us right now, but you live in New York, and tomorrow you're in Baltimore, and I like your dress and your shoes and you seem really sexy and happy, and you seem really into this career that you have. It's all driven by your passion and your purpose, and I'm just trying to figure out, like, how are you doing all this?" And all the other women would clap their hands and be like, "Yeah, mmmhmm, that's what I was trying to figure out, too." And so I came up with this one-liner that I would use whenever I got that question. I would say, "Oh, I just expect far less from myself and way more from my husband than the average woman." And everyone would kind of laugh, and I would try to move them on to what I felt were more substantive questions about women in leadership.

But one day I literally stepped back from the podium and I had what I call a "Tiffany epiphany." It was a voice that said, "Honey, they're not asking you how you manage it all because they care about you. They're asking you how you manage it all because they're trying to figure out, 'How can *I* manage it all?' And if your life's work is advancing women and girls, you owe them a better answer to this question than the one-liner you came up with to get a few laughs and move them on to what you think is more important."

And I decided that I should, that I owed it to them, and that them not having the answer to that question and not being able to sort out all the things that were on their plate was literally stifling their ambition. Because why would you want to take on more when you already feel like you're overwhelmed and you can't do any more?

MS: How did you personally discover that it was okay to "drop the ball"?

TD: I got so overwhelmed that I eventually did start dropping balls . . . not that I was necessarily trying to, and I discovered that the world didn't fall apart. I had never had that experience before because I had always been someone who cared deeply about not dropping balls and had been paranoid about not dropping them. And so it kind of kept them up in the air. You know, that "Oh, you mean the mail can pile up and it can be spilling over my kitchen counter and no one's going to come and arrest me for not paying the parking ticket, and none of my friends are going to divorce me and life can still go on?" That for me was a huge awakening that I wanted more women to have because if there's one thing I feel like we need more practice in, it's just failing publicly. To know that life can still go on.

But for me the biggest ball that I needed to drop was just this huge ball around unrealistic expectations and just doing it all, and ultimately that's the ball I feel like women should drop. In my experience, once I dropped the ball, it really did open up a whole new world of possibilities for what I could attain and what I could achieve, in large part from just engaging the people around me.

I could have sworn to you that before my drop-the-ball journey, there was no one to pick up my balls. No one. And that, ultimately, is what has helped me to flourish at work and in life—this letting go of it. It doesn't mean that I don't ever wash the dishes— it just never occurs to me anymore that it's my *job* to wash the dishes. Or that I'm a bad person or a bad mother or a bad wife or a bad worker because I don't.

MS: That's such a good point. Why is it so hard for women to do that?

TD: I think that the big challenge for women is that, in all fairness to us, we have been socially conditioned to assign our value as human beings to our performance in certain roles.

We begin usually as daughters and it goes on to friend, to student, to worker, maybe to wife, mother. And men have roles, too, but unfortunately women have to put the word "good" in front of all our roles. So we can't just be a daughter—we strive to be a good daughter, right? And a good sister, and a good friend, and a good student, and a good worker. And all of what is required in order to fulfill those roles is far too much work than is humanly possible.

But keep in mind, we've been receiving messages that we should be doing that for our entire lives—from watching the other women in our lives, from popular culture. I personally grew up on *The Cosby Show*, and I thought I was going to grow up to be Clair Huxtable. She was this woman with perfectly coiffed hair, she always had these amazing outfits, her makeup was always perfect, she was strong and witty and smart and insightful. And she has perfectly well-behaved children, and her house is always clean, and in the second season she made partner at a law firm. I mean, how ridiculous is that? But I didn't realize that until my drop-the-ball journey.

MS: What can women do to begin to shift some of these unrealistic gendered beliefs and expectations?

TD: I would say the most important thing that women can do is to just let go on the home front and detach our roles and what is happening on the home front from our value as people. And it doesn't seem logistically feasible, but it's just how you feel. Like when I think about how closely I tied how my children's hair looked to my value as a mother, it's remarkable to me. If my son doesn't have a haircut, if my daughter's hair isn't beautifully braided with her beads, or isn't beautifully twisted, I really feel like my kids are going to be walking down the street and someone's going to look at them and say, "Ooh, who is their mother, and why doesn't she love them?" My husband never has a thought that he's a bad father or that anyone would question who he is because his son needs a haircut. And that's really the tough piece. I have some tools and tips—I talk about delegating with joy; I talk about things like using a management Excel list. But at the end of the day, no tool or tip is going to compensate for your home-control disease until you manage that first.

MS: **For women with children, how can they pass this impor-tant message on to their kids?**

TD: Less words and more modeling. I never, ever remember any-one telling me that I had to do it all. I don't recall anyone ever tell-ing me that I needed to do it perfectly. I just experienced perfectly cornrowed hair. I just experienced my homemade birthday cake. I just experienced that there were never any dirty dishes in the kitchen sink. So I think that the most powerful thing that we could do to disrupt gender expectations on the home front is to model this disruption ourselves, because our children are watching us. And I think that part of the reason why sexism is such an insidious "-ism" to crack is because it's the one "-ism" that close proximity to someone who isn't like you doesn't really help the situation. All of our other "-isms," when you spend time with people from the LGBT community, when you get to know them personally, you become invested in them and their stories and their civil rights. We do this with people of color; we do this across religious lines and ethnicity. But because our gender indoctrination starts so early at home, and because even a staunch feminist like myself for most of her young adulthood was not disrupting that in the home, we were kind of running on default. So I think it's less what we say to our girls and our boys, and it's more what we model for them and what we don't model for them.

MS: You've long been an advocate for gender parity and getting more women into leadership roles, since they're so underrepresented. What's the bigger picture? How is this connected to the wider movement?

TD: It's connected because it has become really clear to me that the unequal division of labor at home literally stifles the ambition of whoever is the primary caregiver. So literally, the person who is washing more clothes at home, washing more dishes, responsible for the runny noses . . . all of that plays into their psyche, quite frankly, whether they're a man or a woman, around what they're going to be capable of in the workplace. And it's part of the reason once women get to middle management, we make a conscious or unconscious decision that this is kind of where we want to hover because we can't take on any more. And we're looking at the C-suite and we're saying, "Hmm, I don't think I really want to do that." So that to me is why I feel like the drop-the-ball message and my book is important because now, more than ever, I just don't feel like we have the luxury of not being leaders. I would love for us to have more women whose bandwidth is freed up, especially psychologically, but also just literally, so that they can aspire to the highest level.

MS: With all of this in mind, how can women best prioritize all the different responsibilities in their lives?

TD: One of the things that is really important is getting clear about what matters most to you. It's the first question I ask women when I connect with them. I meet with at least six or seven women a week. And we just talk—about their lives, about their struggles, about their dilemmas. I try to help them achieve clarity through guidance and encouragement, and I learn a lot from them as well.

The first question I always ask them is, "What matters most to you?" And the reason why it's the most important question is because most of us, unless we've taken the time to intentionally take ourselves through some kind of process of figuring out what matters most to us, we're executing based on what matters most to other people. We're literally living someone else's story. So the first exercise I take them through is getting clear about that.

And, for me, once I got clear that what mattered most to me was advancing women and girls, nurturing a healthy partnership with my husband, and raising conscious global citizens, I then had what I needed to figure out, "What is my highest and best use to achieve what matters most to me?" If what matters most to me is raising conscious global citizens, and I've got scheduling a dentist appointment on my to-do list, is scheduling a dentist appointment my highest and best use in raising conscious global citizens? No! All of a sudden, something that I was stressing over, that I thought if I didn't do meant that I was a terrible person, wasn't very important at all in the scheme of things. [It] doesn't mean that it still doesn't need to get done, but it certainly means that I don't have to do it. [It] definitely doesn't mean that

I'm a bad mother if I don't get around to it. And that's the first step of dropping the ball.

So I talk about what matters most, and then I talk about getting clear about your highest and best use, which is essentially a combination of what you do very well with very little effort. So for me, for example, one of the things I do very well with very little effort is coaching others. One of the things that combines with that is, "What is it that only *you* can do?" One of the things that only I can do in relationship to my kids is instill the values that I want them to learn. It's still very hard to outsource the installation of values. So my highest and best use in raising conscious global citizens is engaging my kids in meaningful conversations every day. Basically, I have coaching conversations with my kids every day about what kind of day they created, about the decisions that they made, about the thoughts they had, about how they interacted with the people in their world. And so, even if I didn't make the dentist appointment, even if I didn't help my daughter sell her Girl Scout cookies, even if I forgot to get the flip-flops for the swimming class, I know that I am doing exactly what I need to be doing every single day to raise conscious global citizens because I did stop for twenty minutes and have a meaningful conversation with them.

12

FIND A MENTOR AND THEN BE A MENTOR

Your life is more enhanced when you can take what you've been given and give to others. The idea is servant leadership, the spirit of Ubuntu—"I am because we are." The idea is using the fullest, highest expression of yourself in such a way that it changes not just you but other people.
—Oprah Winfrey

Mentoring is increasingly seen as one of the most effective and yet underutilized strategies that can help close the gender gap in leadership. Mentoring can help more women advance to the top of their professions, as well as gain access to capital, skills, and career-advancing opportunities they might otherwise not have had.

For me, I have been so fortunate to have some incredibly special mentors, a few of whom are even featured in this book. I consider Gloria Steinem, Pat Mitchell, and Eve Ensler to be among a list of remarkable women who have served as pivotal supporters, cheerleaders, guides, and advisors who have inspired, nurtured, and shaped my career over the past two decades in so many important ways. And I have tried to do the same for many other young women in my life.

These days, there are so many formal and informal ways to connect with a mentor and to become a mentor for someone else (many organizations now offer mentoring events and opportunities), which can be an incredibly rewarding exchange on both ends, and is an actual, meaningful way for women—and men—to help women achieve equity in the workplace and beyond.

Women just need to have somebody to guide them. Everybody needs some kind of mentor to figure out how to navigate what they're trying to get to. People like to hire who they look like—whether you're talking gender or race—and breaking through that can be very, very challenging. Figuring out how you juggle all that and juggle a personal life as well, and a healthy family—I think that's really very hard, and it requires a lot of mentoring. Being great at your job is not enough.

My dearest, best, most supportive cheerleaders in this business are women who really back each other up, all the time. I look at myself, and I look at other women—we're on panels, we're running around, hosting people, mentoring people, sitting down and having lunches with young people. That's what we do. Most of my girlfriends do the same thing that I do, and we do it a lot. We do it right before we run home to pick up our kids from school, or run out to some parent-teacher conference. I see tons of examples of women doing that.

—SOLEDAD O'BRIEN

I look toward older women especially who have navigated motherhood and a career and a sense of self, and I lean on them quite a bit. I'm at a time now in my life where I'm really interested in people older than me who have something to share with me about how they did it.

—AMY POEHLER

think that mentorship and generosity in our careers and in our experiences is often missing from the conversation. And it's not because women don't want to help other women. I think often it's because they have to do so much work to get where they are, that it's almost impossible to think about adding another thing on the pile of things they already have to do. So I think that can be a difficult task, but if we incorporate it as a seamless part of your everyday leadership, it becomes a little bit easier. And I did like what Sheryl Sandberg had to say about mentorship, that it is not just approaching someone and saying, "Will you be my mentor?" and talking to them for an hour, once a week; it's about helping people out along the way and recognizing good work when you see it.

—JESSICA VALENTI

think women my age actually crave mentorship. It's a topic that keeps coming up amongst my friends and amongst other young activists. Older feminists often complain that we're not learning from them or reaching out to them, but at the same time they don't seem to be seeking out mentees, either. I think so many young women would love to learn from older women but don't know how to forge that connection, and that relationship has to be a two-way street.

—JULIE ZEILINGER

When I first opened the [Oprah Winfrey Leadership Academy for Girls], I said to Maya Angelou, "Oh my goodness, this is going to be my legacy." And Maya said, "You have no idea what your legacy is going to be. The truth is your legacy is every life you have ever touched." And that is true for me; it is true for every person who is reading this; it's true for you. The imprint, the heart print, that you leave on every person's life that you're exposed to, that is your real legacy.

It's the most rewarding, fulfilling, and, I would have to say, fun. I have great relationships with all my girls, particularly the seven who are in school in the United States—I speak to them regularly. It has actually enhanced and uplifted my life in ways that I never even imagined, being quote, "Mom Oprah." So the aspect of mothering—it's just turned out to be perfect for me, because I probably wouldn't have been good with little kids, with the life that I was leading, and now they're just at the perfect age so that we can share and experience and have real conversations about things that matter. And I can use my life experience, what I know, to help them become more of who they're meant to be.

—OPRAH WINFREY

I had a fabulous grandmother. And my mother. I have some sister friends. . . . They have influenced and strengthened my life. And when I want to think about what would be the right thing to do, the fair thing to do, the wise thing to do, I can just think of my grandmother. I can always hear her say, "Now, sister, you know what's right. Just do right!"

—MAYA ANGELOU

I think it's important for us to support one another, because your leadership journey is a team sport. It's not a solo endeavor. No one gets to be successful without the investment of other people. And if you operate with that mentality, then it makes perfect sense that you would constantly be recruiting and engaging people to support you in your leadership journey.

—TIFFANY DUFU

I had a significant role model in my life, my grandmother. And I also had many role models that inspired me like Hillary Clinton and other women who achieved great things in their lives.

Hillary has always been one of my best role models and mentors. She was the one who got me off the sidelines! When she gave that speech in China [at the United Nations Fourth World Conference on Women in 1995], not only did she inspire me when she said, "Women's rights are human rights and human rights are women's rights," but the fact that she was so bold in delivering that message from a stage in Beijing really blew me away. At that moment, I said, "I have to get involved in politics."

She was such an important role model to me at that time. And [other women] may be someone's role model, too—they may be the one who gets someone else off the sidelines or provides that great life advice just at the right moment or who gives somebody the guidance they desperately need to take the next steps in their own story.

Hillary has really done that for me on many occasions. But interestingly, in all the times that she gave me advice, it was less than an hour and a half—it wasn't a lot of time! And so it means to me that you don't have to spend a lot of time to help another woman. You don't have to take on the world to make a difference.

—KIRSTEN GILLIBRAND

There is a point, and it's usually around puberty and when you're becoming a woman—that transition time—where women do lose their voice. If we could save them the time lost between that time and the time when they start to regain it, can you imagine the power we would unleash?

It's why most of my work now is in mentoring, because that's a way of doing it one-on-one, one-to-twenty, however I can do it. I spend a lot of time on college campuses, a lot of time mentoring young women in all sectors of business because I don't want them to spend as much time to get their voice as I did.

—PAT MITCHELL

13

ENCOURAGE GIRLS TO BE LEADERS

*It's really important for girls to be reminded that the sky is
the limit, and anything they want to do is possible.*
—Amy Poehler

One of the most common refrains that came up in my interviews about how we can create more women leaders is to
encourage girls to see themselves as leaders in the first place
from early on in their lives. We can all understand why this is so
necessary—girls are continually bombarded in society and by the
media with so many disempowering messages that offer them
limiting narratives on what they can aspire to be. They become
fixated on all the wrong things, like their appearance, their weight,
pleasing others, or being "liked." I can attest to this, since I had
very low self-esteem when I was a young girl. It took me years into
adulthood to discover and utilize my true voice and power.

Now, as the mother of two very empowered daughters with a
strong sense of self, I am heartened to see what is possible when
girls are offered encouragement and positive messages. My girls
have benefited not just from me talking to them candidly about
my own struggles and life lessons I have experienced, but also

from being exposed firsthand to feminist principles and a front-row seat to the many inspiring role models I have been lucky enough to interact with and interview over the years.

Hopefully the following collection of words of wisdom will resonate with the young girl in all of us who still needs encouragement—and offer inspiration about messages we can intentionally instill in the young girls we encounter in our many capacities: as mothers, family members, mentors, educators. Girls are the leaders of our present and future!

For much more on this, see the book I created especially for girls and young women:
Dare to Be You: Inspirational Advice for Girls on Finding Your Voice, Leading Fearlessly, and Making a Difference.

The message I would most want to instill in girls is: you are more powerful than you know; you are beautiful just as you are.

—MELISSA ETHERIDGE

It's not just rhetoric, it is a fact that when you change a girl's life, you affect her vision of herself and her immediate world and the world that she will have an impact on. Because what girls do is they give back. The first thing they want to do is help their brothers and sisters. They help their mothers. Statistics have shown that when you empower a girl, you don't just change that one girl's life—you change the whole family.

—OPRAH WINFREY

Pat Mitchell once asked me at a TED Talk if I were queen of the world, what would I do? What I really would do if I were queen of the world would be [foster] the education of women and girls worldwide because I think that would be the most transformative difference in our society.

—NANCY PELOSI

It starts young: girls are discouraged from leading at an early age. The word "bossy" is largely applied to girls, not boys. I think we need to expect and encourage our girls and women to lead and contribute.

—SHERYL SANDBERG

As I now move into the grandmother phase, I see that the three- and four-year-old girls are punished for being aggressive, and the boys, "Well, that's the way that boys are." So I think if you start getting put down when you're three, it sort of sets it up for the rest of your life. And I shake my head when, even at three, they categorize themselves into the pink category and blue is for boys, which is representative of so much: that they want to be pink to be acceptable. It's hard to go against that grain, but I think we must; we must give our children all kinds of toys and let them be who they are and support and encourage them.

—CAROL JENKINS

We have to actually trust girls and stop telling them that they have to be someone other than who they are. One of the things I'm discovering is that the more girls feel confident in themselves, the more they are able to express who they really are. I think we have to find situations where girls find their own voices. We have to help girls find activities that fulfill their deepest selves. If you live in a society that tells you your whole point is to be pretty and skinny, then you'll spend your days working to achieve that. But if you're brought up in a world that tells you that your point is to make the world better and to contribute and to transform consciousness, then you will go and work on achieving that.

—EVE ENSLER

I read a study when I was in college about how in the United States, if you see class president elections, it's like all girls [run] until eighth grade, and then no girls run. What happens in there that tells girls to be quiet, be submissive, be meek? It's ridiculous—we're missing out on 50 percent of our potential great people.

—NATALIE PORTMAN

At the age of seven, like 30 percent across the board, boys and girls want to be president. And then at the age of thirteen, the numbers completely skew. You have one girl for every nine guys that want to be president.

At ages ten to twelve, girls learn patriarchy. They learn their place in the world. They learn that there isn't a seat for them at the table, that they aren't the natural-born leaders. I mean, that's not truthful, but that's what they're taught, that's what our society has constructed, so to speak. Boys at four and five are learning patriarchy, they're learning hierarchy, the alpha male, the top dog.

I want so badly to shift this and create a healthier culture. We as parents and as teachers and as educators in all forms . . . we're so stuck in what we've accepted as normal: this is what it is to be a man; this is what it is to be a woman. And it's increasingly been pushed to extremes vis-à-vis media, which perpetuate it, and capitalism, which is all about sell, sell, sell. We're creating a very painful and lonely existence for both our men and our women.

—JENNIFER SIEBEL NEWSOM

This is proven time and time again: girls do what they see, not what they're told. So I think the more that you can expose them to examples of people *doing*—especially women, but equally expose them to men who are taking on child-rearing and men who are leaving work at five o'clock and women who are doing the things that sort of defy stereotypes—then that exposure is going to become so valuable. . . . And the more you can expose them both in personal and professional ways to those differences, the more that's going to become their sense of normalcy and the more they can see women in positions of power from early on.

—AMY RICHARDS

We can't have true equality for girls if they never see themselves in penultimate leadership positions. And it isn't just a question of not seeing a woman as president: not seeing a woman as the leading general or leader of any of the major branches of the military; not seeing a woman governor in their state, ever; not seeing a woman head of a major company in their state; not seeing a woman mayor of the major city in their state. This really influences how they see themselves, so it has a profound impact on what girls think is possible for themselves.

—CELINDA LAKE

From the point of view of my generation, I think visibility is so important in inspiring future generations of leaders. We can't be what we can't see, essentially. If we don't see female politicians out there in equal numbers to men, then going into politics, or leadership in general, doesn't seem like a viable option for us.

—JULIE ZEILINGER

When I was a child, we were raised with my grandfather and my dad, who was in the military. And my grandfather would get furious if I ever acted like I couldn't do something because I was a girl. He was like, "You're just as good as those boys. What's wrong with you?" And my mother would say, "So what if there's a boy trying to beat you in this or that? You better study hard so you can beat this guy and make a better grade than that boy next door."

So thank goodness my family were feminists, even the men in my family, at an early age. Not every girl has that kind of encouragement early on. And so I think what is important is that at an early age, young girls have an educational environment and the family support systems in place where everything is equal to boys and that they're told early on that there is no difference in terms of their abilities and their intellectual capabilities and their opportunities. This has to be taught early. And then we have to make sure that the opportunities are there and that we *don't* discriminate against those girls and we *do* have what it takes for girls to succeed in school.

I fortunately went to an all-women's college, which was great. By the time I got to Mills College, I was so far ahead of most of my counterparts and my friends in school because I had had this upbringing. But the support that was there for me as a young girl and as a teenager and a young mom and all, it was just always, "You're no different from this guy in terms of your ability or capacity. Just work hard and know that you're going to hit some ceilings that you've got to shatter."

—BARBARA LEE

The most important message that I give to young kids and to people I meet across my state, across the country, is that their voices matter. This is a moment in time where we cannot stay silent, that we must speak up. . . . You have to fight back, you have to speak out. You have to do whatever your time and talents will allow you to do to make a difference.

—KIRSTEN GILLIBRAND

Civic education can and must happen alongside other changes that might need to be addressed. Today's students will determine the future of our society and our institutions, and we cannot wait to educate them about civic participation until we think conditions have been perfected. They will be the ones who will need to take the reins to continue to perfect our union, and they must be educated to do so.

—SANDRA DAY O'CONNOR

Girls and women face many challenges in achieving equality with men and boys. In education, access to justice, property rights, health services, politics, business—in almost every aspect of life, women are treated differently and often worse than men, and girls are often given fewer opportunities than boys. As Elders [a group of global leaders who work together for peace and human rights], we are fully committed to the principle that all human beings are of equal worth. We highlight equality for girls and women, not just women's rights. That is important, [because] girls, especially adolescent girls, have been almost invisible in debates on equal rights. Yet it is in adolescence that events can have a huge effect on a girl's life.

—MARY ROBINSON

At the Girls Leadership Institute, the organization that I cofounded, what we argue is that relationships are a classroom for leadership in girls' lives. So we try to give girls the skills to tell their friends how they are feeling, promote their own perspective, negotiate, compromise, advocate for themselves—and in doing that, build the skills that they will then, hopefully, import with them into a work or leadership setting. That to me is the intervention.

—RACHEL SIMMONS

Young women really need role models. It cannot just be about the Kardashians or music stars. Ultimately, young women need to be shown women of achievement, women of courage, women of stature, women of dignity who are doing things for the world.

—TINA BROWN

Each [girl] is already a unique and valuable person when she's born; every human being is. Inside each of us is a unique person resulting from millennia of environment and heredity combined in a way that could never happen again and could never have happened before.

—GLORIA STEINEM

We need [girls] to really internalize the message that good enough is good enough. You don't need to be perfect. We're not supposed to be perfect; we're supposed to be complete. And you can't be complete if you're trying to be perfect.

—JANE FONDA

14

LIFT UP MARGINALIZED VOICES

What you deny someone else, you are denying yourself.
And what you deny yourself, you are denying someone
else.
—Melissa Etheridge

The notion of moving from hierarchical power *over* to more inclusive power *to* comes up frequently when I ask people about what women in positions of power might do differently. Now more than ever, there is a sense of the absolute necessity of using our power and leadership to uplift, amplify, and support marginalized voices—those whose needs and perspectives are often not adequately represented or heard in our politics and society. There is a fresh awareness of the imperative of having movements become more "intersectional" and taking into account our multiple identities. The dictionary definition of "intersectionality" (coined by civil rights advocate and scholar Kimberlé Crenshaw) is "the complex, cumulative way in which the effects of multiple forms of discrimination (such as racism, sexism, and classism) combine, overlap, or intersect especially in the experiences of marginalized individuals or groups." In other words, you simply cannot uproot one system of oppression without addressing them all and working together.

As more women are coming into leadership, my hope is that we can model how we can use our power and influence to represent those who do not yet have an equal voice or who are relegated to feeling powerless or invisible in our society. We all benefit from a more diverse, equal, and just world.

The most important [leadership quality] is the ability to connect with the problems of people who are not like you—those who have been underserved by government historically, who don't enjoy the privileges that you do. So the ability to really connect with those people and design policies that will include their well-being—with an understanding that as they go, so goes the rest of the country—I think that is important and may be the most critical characteristic of a leader today. Because so often those are the people who are not going to be represented by a lobbyist or a very important vocal donor, so those are the interests that can get lost.

—ANITA HILL

As a woman, I'm a minority—and once other people's rights start getting taken away, it's a step toward taking mine away. So I have to try to protect the rights of others. It's impossible for me to think of injustice, oppression, discrimination, and non-freedom as not having to do with me—it totally has to do with me.

Things being right affects us all—caring that we live in a just world, no matter what. You can't separate yourself; no matter how much money you have, no matter how famous you are, no matter how religious you are, no matter how great a job you have, you are affected by the injustices of the world. You are, no matter what.

—KATHY NAJIMY

I'll never forget my very first few months at Planned Parenthood. I went to the Supreme Court. We had a major case to argue, and

sitting there in the audience and seeing—because it's such an inti-
mate, small space—this tiny, fierce woman, Ruth Bader Ginsburg,
was holding on her shoulders the entire population of women in
this country. And of course, it was a choice issue, so she was trying
to represent all of us. It was so stunning; it made me realize how
other disenfranchised groups have felt all their lives of not being
represented in the highest court in the land. There is a lot more
that we have to do, and it's up to us to do it.

—CECILE RICHARDS

If you have a person enslaved, the first thing you must do is to
convince yourself that the person is subhuman and won't mind
the enslavement. The second thing you must do is convince your
allies that the person is subhuman, so that you have some support.
But the third and the unkindest cut of all is to convince that person that he or she is not quite a first-class citizen. When the complete job has been done, the initiator can go back years later and
ask, "Why don't you people like yourselves more?" You see? It's
been true for women, it's been true for immigrants, it's been true
for Asians, it's been true for Spanish-speaking people. So now we
have to undo. We can learn to see each other and see ourselves in
each other and recognize that human beings are more alike than
we are unalike.

If you decide, "I will not stay in rooms where women are belittled; I will not stay in company where races, no matter who they
are, are belittled; I will not take it; I will not sit around and accept
dehumanizing other human beings"—if you decide to do that in
small ways, and you continue to do it—finally you realize you've

got so much courage. Imagine it: you've got so much courage that people want to be around you. They get a feeling that they will be protected in your company.

People are saying, "This is what I will stand for. And I will not stand for any less than this." It's amazing. We are growing up! We are growing up out of the idiocies—racism and sexism and ageism and all those ignorances.

—MAYA ANGELOU

You can get courage from the people you're fighting for. Any time I get discouraged and I sit down with some of the constituents or women who are suffering, who need my voice—when I see their courage to tell their stories—it gives me the courage to then elevate their stories and to fight even harder for them.

—KIRSTEN GILLIBRAND

My message really is that your work needs to be for everybody. I think women should rise up, not just because our rights are being violated, but because when our rights are recognized and supported and upheld, everybody's are.

—JODY WILLIAMS

I do feel that we are in desperate enough straits right now that those of us who have resources—not just money, but other kinds of know-how—need to step forward and put those resources to work where people are vulnerable.

I have trouble with some of the events that I go to that congratulate women, give them opportunities to network, leverage the power that they have to have more power. I feel they could do more, and I feel they *need* to do more because what we're asking disenfranchised women to do is a lot more with fewer resources. I would like women in power in this country to do a lot more than they're doing to help others. It doesn't make me feel that great to go to events which are just about "them" getting more resources to climb. I would say to women, "As you reach up, please reach out."

—ANNA DEAVERE SMITH

We are all interconnected, and women here need to know what women are facing in different countries. I feel that the more we learn about the world, the more we understand ourselves.

—TINA BROWN

It's a sisterhood that has to come together. When our sisters speak truth, we have to make sure that they are respected for the truth that they speak.

—NANCY PELOSI

If you have any degree of success and if you can use that success to give exposure to people and financial help, then that's a wonderful thing to do.

—DIANE VON FURSTENBERG

Trust your own outrage. I think my parents did a really incredible job of making me know that my emotional reactions to the world or to ideas or to other people were valid and valuable. . . . There was respect for the idea that when your gut tells you something is wrong, you trust that—and that it's not just for you. It's for other people who might not be able to speak as loudly or as clearly as you might be able to. Part of your responsibility as just a person who cares about people is to trust your own outrage and speak out about it.

—COURTNEY E. MARTIN

15

JOIN FORCES WITH OTHER WOMEN

Sisters: talk to each other, be connected and informed,
form women's circles, share your stories, work together,
and take risks. Together we are invincible. There is
nothing to be afraid of.
—Isabel Allende

There is so much strength to be harnessed when women join forces. Now more than ever, women are finding ways to come together and share our collective power and strength. Whether it is millions of us marching together around the world in unified protest and solidarity at the Women's March, bravely sharing our stories online to create accountability and change through #MeToo, supporting women candidates who are running for office, or coming together in smaller circles, conferences, and gatherings to listen and learn and offer encouragement and support to each other, we are our most transformative force when we are linked.

Though our culture often tries to pit women and girls against each other, or to be competitive, we have to resist that inclination since we all suffer when we operate from a place of scarcity, competition, or isolation. Through my work over the decades in the women's space and through my platforms Feminist.com and What Will It Take, I have participated in and helped to organize many events and think tanks bringing women leaders and advocacy organizations together to talk about how we can better coordinate, share information and tools, and work together toward common goals. I find that it is mostly a misconception that women do not want to form these connections; they do. But there aren't enough opportunities to help facilitate these types of collaborative conversations and strategizing. We have to reach out intentionally when we need help or support, and offer it up when we have an opportunity. We have to learn to see other women's success as our success.

The power of sisterhood is one of our greatest strengths and the fuel to help us get to where we want to go—both individually and collectively—faster. We know that progress toward gender equality has been slow, but now there are so many pressing and urgent reasons why this country and the world need more women leaders—and women's voices, ideas, and stories—to be heard. Now is the time to join forces so we can dramatically move the needle toward building the future that we want for ourselves and for generations to come.

I always think it's important for communities to join forces. You hear everybody talk about the importance of being a part of a network, a part of knowing that there are women out there who are thinking like you and moving like you and organizing like you, and who understand what you're going through. Ram Dass talks about the illusion of aloneness, and I think that's what we all fall into sometimes—as women, as people of color, as educators, as organizers—this illusion that we're trying to do this all alone or that we'll never make a difference. Coming together is what allows us to keep moving forward.

It's so important that [women] look each other in the eye and go, "What's happening is not okay, and we are not alone in trying to shift it. We are not alone in our pain, and we are not alone in our transforming our pain into power. We're all doing it, and we support each other in doing it."

—KERRY WASHINGTON

I advocate that every woman be a part of a circle that meets at least once a month or, if you can't do that, once every two months or every four months. But you have to have a circle, a group of people—smart, wise, can-do women—who are in the world doing their work, and you need to meet with them as often as you can so that they can see what you're doing and who you are, and you can see the same. And you can talk to each other about the world and about your lives in a circle of trust and safety. It's crucial for our psychological health and our spiritual growth. It's essential.

—ALICE WALKER

We're seeing right now what happens when not only we women speak out on an individual level—[we also see] the power of community, the power of many voices, the truths about sexual assault, sexual harassment that had been buried for so long, not just because women had strong reasons to not speak out, but because of patriarchy and misogyny. Those kinds of massive institutions of injustice and habits of injustice don't topple because we kind of hope they will. It happens when we all come together, speak up, support those who do, sometimes yell really loudly as a group— women and men, using their voices collectively for justice. And I think certainly in recent history, we're seeing day after day after day the ripple effects of what happens when more women speak out together and act to make change. We're seeing how incredibly powerful and persuasive that is.

—SALLY KOHN

When women get together as a group, it's immensely powerful.

—ANNIE LENNOX

I think we need to continue as women to constantly celebrate what we have in common and share—and stop letting society focus on how we're different.

—AMY POEHLER

I learned the power of the word "we." Not saying to people, "You are going to get through this," but, "*We* are going to get through this." That is such a different message, because it makes people feel less alone, and [in] all of these forms of hardship, it's not just the hardship itself but the isolation that comes with it. "We" changes that.

—SHERYL SANDBERG

We can see—from California to New York, from Maine to Florida, Seattle to New Mexico—everywhere there are women's groups. Everywhere there are women who have gotten together to examine global warming and women who have gotten together to prepare each other for single parenting, women who have come together to be supportive—all sorts of gatherings of women. That's very heartening.

—MAYA ANGELOU

We're given a lot of messages about our own worth from a lot of different places that aren't aligned with what's real. Creating community and safe spaces with other women, where we can share our stories and people can recognize that they're not alone, is absolutely essential. When you realize that you might not be the only one who goes through these things, it builds and strengthens a sense of humanity and a sense of, "It isn't just me. There's a larger thing happening, and I actually have some agency and ability to do something about it. And I have these people who will stand with me as I try."

You can cultivate courage on your own, but a lot of courage happens through connection and relationship with others. For me, it's been incredibly inspiring to bear witness to women who, against all odds, assert the dignity of their work and their right to be recognized for the work that they do for families. That takes so much courage and is a huge source of inspiration and strength. At the end of the day, all of us need other people to inspire us and give us strength.

We have to show up for each other, we have to contribute to each other's campaigns, we have to mobilize one another. We have to really put our actions where our aspirations are and follow, support, and invest in women. We're in this historic moment where, it's kind of like every few generations, there is a social movement moment that fundamentally redefines and re-updates our democracy. And like the civil rights movement before, we're actually in this moment where we can make our democracy, as a whole, work better, and the way to get there is through women's leadership, women's activism. There's no doubt that women are the cutting edge of this next opportunity to improve and strengthen our democracy. The thing is, we only get there if we invest in and support and add oxygen to every single act of courage and organizing that's happening among women. We have to take responsibility ourselves for realizing the opportunity of this movement moment.

—AI-JEN POO

When women do decide to run, we have to support them. Women have to support other women, and we also need to bring in a coalition of willing men to recognize that it is in *their* interest to have our voices at the table. This isn't just for women; this is for our entire society. I think we all have to roll up our sleeves, we have to get behind candidates who reflect our values, we have to work hard.

—VALERIE JARRETT

Getting women to run is important, and being there for women politicians in a way that is really loud and clear. Not forgetting once they win. We need to tweet and email and call and fax and use whatever means of communication—carrier pigeon, if necessary—when they have bills up that we approve of. We need to become less apathetic and more involved.

—ROBIN MORGAN

I think that it is very important for women to help each other. It is hard to be the only woman in the room. Having a support system is very important. When I was in office, I had a group of women foreign ministers that were my friends throughout the world.

So I think there has to be a sense that once you have climbed the ladder of success, that you don't push it away from the building— you are only strengthened if there are more women.

—MADELEINE ALBRIGHT

Washington is certainly broken, but the one area of exception, in my opinion, is among the women. We have these quarterly dinners. We get together as people first—as wives and mothers and sisters and daughters. And we talk about our shared interests, our shared values, things that we want to achieve for our children.

And it's a really special place, because the partisan politics really have no place there.

—KIRSTEN GILLIBRAND

If women have confidence in themselves, they will have confidence in other women. Sometimes we wonder, what is the support of women, for women? Sometimes I think it's because, "Well, I can do that. Why is *she* doing it?" You know, it's not a zero-sum game—there's plenty of opportunity for everyone, so there's no reason to worry about somebody else's success, either saying you couldn't do this so she's better than you, or she's doing it so you can't. No, she's doing it so you *can*.

—NANCY PELOSI

I hope in the future, feminism is about women increasingly supporting each other. As I was moving up in my career, I could almost *hear* the women coming up behind me. I could almost hear them coming up. And I knew they were cheering, because I knew that every time I made a space for me, I made a space for them. When you think about that, you're stronger—you can face what comes at you, because you know that you're not alone. And we are not alone. When we stand up for ourselves, we stand up for all the women around us.

—ANN CURRY

It's important to cultivate relationships, particularly with other women. We need to build networks or friendships with women that are trust-based and that also have a strong contemplative, functional, and instrumental aspect. Many of my teaching collaborations are with extraordinary women who have matured, gone through many difficulties, who have great wisdom, humor, and compassion, and are vigorous and committed. . . . Through partnership and collaboration with other women, we have a phenomenal capacity to consume less and give more to our children, our communities, and the world.

—JOAN HALIFAX

If we're by ourselves, we come to feel crazy and alone. We need to make alternate families of small groups of women who support each other, talk to each other regularly, can speak their truths and their experiences and find they're not alone in them—that other women have them, too. It makes such a huge difference.

—GLORIA STEINEM

When we pull ourselves together and focus on what we want, there is nothing holding women back. It's beautiful when we see it happen. It is exponential, the power that women feel when they are joined together in common purpose.

—CECILE RICHARDS

BIOGRAPHIES

Luvvie Ajayi is a bestselling author, speaker, digital strategist, and veteran blogger. She is executive director and cofounder of The Red Pump Project, a national nonprofit that educates women and girls of color about HIV/AIDS. She is also the author of the *New York Times* bestseller *I'm Judging You: The Do-Better Manual.*

Madeleine Albright, PhD, served as US Ambassador to the United Nations and went on to become the first woman to hold the position of US Secretary of State. She is a professor at Georgetown University and the author of several bestselling books.

Isabel Allende—novelist, feminist, and philanthropist—is one of the most widely read authors in the world, having sold more than seventy-four million books. In addition to her work as a writer, she devotes much of her time to human rights causes. She is the founder of the Isabel Allende Foundation, which invests in the power of women and girls to secure reproductive rights, economic independence, and freedom from violence.

Dr. Maya Angelou, 1928–2014, was an accomplished poet, award-winning writer, performer, dancer, actress, director, and teacher. She was also an activist for social causes and civil rights, which included organizing with Dr. Martin Luther King Jr., marching for women's rights with Gloria Steinem, and lobbying on behalf of marriage equality.

India.Arie is an R&B singer-songwriter, producer, and philanthropist. She has received four Grammy Awards, twenty-one Grammy nominations, and has sold ten million albums worldwide. In 2008, she launched her own music label, SoulBird Music. She has also worked steadily throughout her career to champion causes close to her heart. She has traveled to Africa numerous times to address the AIDS crisis.

Kelly Ayotte served as Republican US senator for New Hampshire from 2011 to 2017. Prior to her time in office, she was a longtime prosecutor and New Hampshire's first female attorney general. She now serves on the board of directors of Winning For Women.

Joy Behar is a comedian, writer, actor, and cohost of *The View*. She has hosted several of her own TV shows, including *The Joy Behar Show* and *Joy Behar: Say Anything!* She is the author of a number of books, including *When You Need a Lift: But Don't Want to Eat Chocolate, Pay a Shrink, or Drink a Bottle of Gin* and, most recently, *The Great Gasbag: An A-to-Z Study Guide to Surviving Trump World*.

Carol Moseley Braun served as Democratic US senator for Illinois from 1993 to 1999 and was the first African American woman to be elected to the US Senate. In 2003, she campaigned for the

Democratic presidential nomination. She is also a civil rights and women's rights activist.

Donna Brazile is a veteran Democratic political strategist and activist, adjunct professor, author, syndicated columnist, political commentator, and vice chair of voter registration and participation at the Democratic National Committee.

Tina Brown is an award-winning writer and editor, founder of the Women in the World Summit, president and CEO of Tina Brown Live Media, and founder of The Daily Beast. Between 1979 and 1998 she was the editor of *Tatler, Vanity Fair*, and *The New Yorker*. She is also the author of *The Vanity Fair Diaries*, which chronicles her years as the editor in chief of *Vanity Fair*.

Tarana Burke is a civil rights activist and the original founder of the #MeToo movement, which she started in 2006. In 2017, the movement blossomed into a worldwide campaign to raise awareness about sexual harassment, abuse, and assault.

Sophia Bush is an actress, activist, director, and producer. She starred as Brooke Davis in the WB/CW drama series *One Tree Hill*. From 2014 to 2017, she starred in the NBC police procedural drama series *Chicago P.D.* She is an advocate for women's rights, LGBTQ rights, and encourages people to get politically engaged and vote.

Margaret Cho is a stand-up comedian, actress, bestselling author, activist, singer, and blogger. She has won numerous awards for her efforts to promote equal rights for all people, regardless of race, sexual orientation, or gender identity.

Ann Curry is a former NBC News national and international correspondent and former cohost of the *TODAY* show. She is the head of her own production company, Ann Curry, Inc, through which she recently produced the PBS series *We'll Meet Again*. The winner of seven national news Emmy awards and the recipient of numerous humanitarian awards, she has been recognized for her coverage of global conflicts, nuclear tensions, humanitarian crises, and groundbreaking journalism on climate change.

Susan David, PhD, is an award-winning psychologist on faculty at Harvard Medical School, the cofounder and codirector of the Institute of Coaching at McLean Hospital, CEO of Evidence Based Psychology, an in-demand speaker and consultant, and author of the bestselling book *Emotional Agility*.

Cameron Diaz is a former model who became one of the most sought-after and highest-paid actresses. She has starred in numerous films, including *The Mask, Charlie's Angels, There's Something About Mary, Bad Teacher*, and many others. She is also a devoted environmentalist and the coauthor of the *New York Times* bestsellers *The Body Book* and *The Longevity Book*.

Abigail Disney is an activist, philanthropist, and Emmy Award–winning documentary filmmaker. She is the founder and president of Fork Films and its sister organization, Peace is Loud, which are committed to promoting peace, lifting marginalized voices, and highlighting the stories of women who are stepping up for peace and resisting violence in their communities. In 2018, she partnered with Killer Content to form Level Forward, an entertainment company driving industry and economic transformation through creatively excellent, multiplatform storytelling, which focuses on backing projects driven by women and people of color.

Tiffany Dufu is a catalyst-at-large in the world of women's leadership and the author of *Drop the Ball: Achieving More by Doing Less*, a memoir and manifesto that shows women how to cultivate the single skill they really need in order to thrive: the ability to let go. She is also the founder and CEO of The Cru, a peer coaching platform for women looking to accelerate their professional and personal growth.

Dr. Sylvia Earle is a legendary oceanographer, explorer, author, and lecturer. She has been a National Geographic Society explorer in residence since 1998 and is the founder, president, and chairman of Mission Blue: The Sylvia Earle Alliance, which inspires action to explore and protect the ocean. She is also the director of several corporate and nonprofit organizations.

Eve Ensler is an internationally acclaimed Tony Award–winning playwright, performer, and activist, as well as the author of *The Vagina Monologues*. She is the founder and artistic director of V-Day, the global movement to end violence against women and girls. She is the author of several books, including *I Am an Emotional Creature*, *In the Body of the World*, and, most recently, *The Apology*.

Melissa Etheridge is one of rock music's great female icons, as well as a human rights activist. She is a two-time Grammy winner, multiplatinum recording artist, and 2007 Oscar winner for Best Original Song for "I Need to Wake Up," which she wrote for the documentary *An Inconvenient Truth*.

Gloria Feldt is the cofounder and president of Take The Lead, whose mission is to bring women to parity in leadership positions across all sectors of work and civic life by 2025. She is the former president and CEO of Planned Parenthood, bestselling author of *No Excuses: 9 Ways Women Can Change How We Think About Power*, and teaches Women, Power, and Leadership at Arizona State University.

Sally Field is a two-time Academy Award– and three-time Emmy Award–winning actor who has portrayed dozens of iconic roles on both the large and small screens. She is also a producer, director, and the author of *In Pieces*, her bestselling memoir. In 2012, she was inducted into the American Academy of Arts and Sciences, and in 2015 she was honored by President Obama with the National Medal of Arts.

Eileen Fisher is a fashion designer and the founder and chairwoman of EILEEN FISHER, Inc., which she began in 1984 with $350 in her bank account and not knowing how to sew. Now, thirty-five years later, EILEEN FISHER has stores across the US, UK, and Canada. The Eileen Fisher Foundation and the Eileen Fisher Community Foundation support programs for women and girls worldwide. She is the cocreator of the Eileen Fisher Leadership Institute, a nonprofit that supports leadership in young women through self-empowerment, connection with others, and activism in their communities.

Jane Fonda is an Academy Award–winning actress, bestselling author, and an activist and advocate for environmental issues, human rights, and the empowerment of women and girls. She is a cofounder of the Women's Media Center, which works to make women and girls more visible and powerful in media. Fonda also stars in Netflix's hit series *Grace and Frankie.*

Tulsi Gabbard is a Democratic US representative serving the people of Hawaii's Second Congressional District since 2013 and is the first Hindu woman to be elected to Congress. An advocate for environmental policy, Tulsi ran for the Hawaii State Legislature in 2002 and became the youngest person ever elected. She also served in the armed forces. In 2019, she announced her run for president in 2020.

Melinda Gates is a philanthropist, businesswoman, and global advocate for women and girls. She is co-chair of the Bill & Melinda Gates Foundation, the largest private foundation in the world. She is the author of *The Moment of Lift: How Empowering Women Changes the World.*

Kirsten Gillibrand is a Democratic US senator representing New York. After first being elected to the House of Representatives in 2006, Kirsten Gillibrand was appointed to serve in the seat vacated by Hillary Clinton in January 2009. She won reelection in 2018 with 67 percent of the vote. She is the founder of the Off The Sidelines initiative to get more women civically engaged, and is the author of *Off the Sidelines* and *Bold & Brave*. In 2019, she announced her run for president in 2020.

Carol Gilligan, PhD, is a writer, activist, university professor at NYU, and the author of the landmark book *In a Different Voice*, which transformed psychological theory and feminist thinking. As a member of the Harvard faculty for more than thirty years, she held the university's first chair in Gender Studies. In 1996, she was named by *Time* magazine as one of the twenty-five most influential people. With her graduate students at NYU, she founded the Radical Listening Project. Her latest book, coauthored with Naomi Snider, is *Why Does Patriarchy Persist?*

Dr. Jane Goodall is a world-renowned primatologist, speaker, and author. She founded the Jane Goodall Institute, a global wildlife and environmental conservation organization, as well as Roots & Shoots, a global nonprofit that empowers youths to make a positive difference for all living things.

Joan Halifax is a Buddhist teacher, Zen priest, author, anthropologist, and pioneer in the field of end-of-life care. She is founder, abbot, and head teacher of Upaya Institute and Zen Center in Santa Fe, New Mexico.

Thich Nhat Hanh is a Vietnamese Buddhist monk, peace activist, teacher of the art of mindful living, and the author of many books, including the bestselling *The Miracle of Mindfulness*.

He was nominated for the Nobel Peace Prize by Martin Luther King Jr.

Melissa Harris-Perry is the Maya Angelou Presidential Chair at Wake Forest University and the founding director of the Anna Julia Cooper Center. She is also the former host of MSNBC's program *Melissa Harris-Perry*, an award-winning author, founder and codirector of the innovative bipartisan program Wake the Vote, editor-at-large for Elle.com, and cofounder of Perry Political Partnership, a political consulting business.

Goldie Hawn is an Academy Award–winning actress and founder of The Hawn Foundation, a charity whose signature program, MindUP, helps children develop the mental fitness necessary to thrive in school and throughout their lives. She is the author of *10 Mindful Minutes* and *Goldie: A Lotus Grows in the Mud*.

Anita Hill is an attorney, professor at Brandeis University, and chair of the Hollywood entertainment industry's Commission on Eliminating Sexual Harassment and Advancing Equality. In 1991, her testimony about sexual harassment at the Senate confirmation hearings of Clarence Thomas gained national exposure. She is the author of *Reimagining Equality: Stories of Gender, Race, and Finding Home* and her autobiography, *Speaking Truth to Power*.

Dolores Huerta is a civil rights activist, labor leader, and community organizer who has made it her life's work to advocate for the working poor, women, and children. She cofounded the National Farm Workers Association with César Chávez and is founder and president of the Dolores Huerta Foundation, which creates leadership opportunities for community organizing, civic engagement, and policy advocacy.

Arianna Huffington founded and is the former president and editor in chief of *The Huffington Post*. She is the founder and CEO of Thrive Global, an organization that helps individuals, companies, and communities improve their well-being and performance and unlock their greatest potential. She is the author of fifteen books, including *Thrive: The Third Metric to Redefining Success and Creating a Life of Well-Being, Wisdom, and Wonder* and *The Sleep Revolution: Transforming Your Life, One Night at a Time*.

Kay Bailey Hutchison is the US ambassador to NATO and was the first woman elected to represent Texas in the US Senate, which she did from 1993 to 2013, as a member of the Republican party. She is also a bestselling author of three books: *Unflinching Courage: Pioneering Women Who Shaped Texas*; *American Heroines: The Spirited Women Who Shaped Our Country*; and *Leading Ladies: American Trailblazers*.

Valerie Jarrett is a businesswoman, lawyer, and advocate for equity and justice. She was senior advisor to President Barack Obama during his eight years in office. She is the author of *Finding My Voice: My Journey to the West Wing and the Path Forward*.

Carol Jenkins is co-president and CEO of the ERA Coalition/ Fund for Women's Equality. She is an award-winning writer, producer, and media consultant. She is also a sought-after speaker and writer on issues relating to the media, specifically the participation and inclusion of women and people of color. She was founding president of the Women's Media Center.

Donna Karan is a renowned fashion designer and philanthropist who launched Donna Karan New York, DKNY, and, most recently, Urban Zen, a lifestyle brand and foundation that addresses wellness, education, and the preservation of culture through artisan communities. She is the author of *My Journey*, her memoir.

Billie Jean King is a tennis legend, winning thirty-nine Grand Slam titles, including a record twenty titles at Wimbledon, and defeating male opponent Bobby Riggs in the "Battle of the Sexes" match. She is also a longtime champion for social justice, gender justice, and equality. King founded the Women's Sports Foundation in 1974, a powerful organization dedicated to ensuring all girls have equal access to sports, as well as the Billie Jean King Leadership Initiative in 2014, aimed at achieving diverse, inclusive leadership in the workforce.

Sally Kohn is a political commentator and columnist who frequently appears on CNN, MSNBC, and Fox News. She is the author of *The Opposite of Hate: A Field Guide to Repairing Our Humanity* and host of the *State of Resistance* podcast. Her three TED Talks have been viewed more than four million times.

Nicholas Kristof is a *New York Times* columnist, two-time Pulitzer Prize winner, and coauthor of *A Path Appears: Transforming Lives, Creating Opportunity* and *Half the Sky: Turning Oppression* *into Opportunity for Women Worldwide*, a *New York Times* best-selling book about the challenges facing women around the globe.

Celinda Lake is one of the Democratic party's leading political pollsters and strategists. She is the president of Lake Research Partners, a Democratic polling firm. Her interviews and statistics have been quoted in *The Washington Post*, *The New York Times*, and *The Wall Street Journal*, as well as a variety of magazines, including *Newsweek*, *Glamour*, and *Marie Claire*. Celinda has appeared on numerous television and radio news programs, including CNN, MSNBC, CNBC, Fox News, and NPR, discussing her work and providing expert commentary.

Barbara Lee is a Democratic US representative serving the people of California's Thirteenth Congressional District since 1998. She has long advocated for legislative action for ending poverty, as well as for ending HIV and ensuring an AIDS-free generation.

Annie Lennox is a singer-songwriter, campaigner, and activist. She has sold more than eighty million records and has won countless awards, including four Grammys, a Golden Globe, and an Academy Award. She is the founder of SING, a humanitarian organization that raises awareness for the HIV/AIDS pandemic in Africa.

Elizabeth Lesser is the cofounder and senior advisor of Omega Institute, the largest adult education center in the US focusing on health, wellness, spirituality, social change, and creativity. She is the cofounder of the Omega Women's Leadership Center, which grew out of the popular Women & Power conference series featuring women leaders, activists, authors, and artists from around the world. She is also a bestselling author whose books include *The Seeker's Guide*, *Broken Open*, and *Marrow*.

Wangari Maathai, 1940–2011, was the first African woman to win the Nobel Peace Prize. She founded the Green Belt Movement, a nonprofit organization that has planted more than fifty-one million trees across Kenya. She also cofounded the Nobel Women's Initiative and authored four books.

Courtney E. Martin is a blogger, speaker, facilitator, and the author/editor of five books. She writes frequently for *The New York Times* and *BRIGHT Magazine,* among other publications. Courtney is also the cofounder of the Solutions Journalism Network and FRESH Speakers, Inc., and has consulted with a wide variety of organizations—like TED, the Aspen Institute, the Obama Foundation, and the Sundance Institute—on how to make impactful, story-rich social change.

Claire McCaskill served as a Democratic US senator from Missouri from 2007 to 2019 and was the first female candidate to be elected senator for Missouri. She recently joined NBC News and MSNBC as a political analyst. She is the author of *Plenty Ladylike: A Memoir*.

Pat Mitchell is a groundbreaking media icon, global advocate for women's rights, and cofounder and curator of TEDWomen. She was formerly the president and CEO of PBS and was the first woman to hold that position. She is the author of *Becoming a Dangerous Woman: Embracing Risk to Change the World*.

Robin Morgan is an award-winning poet, novelist, journalist, activist, and bestselling author. She is the former editor in chief of *Ms.* magazine, founder of the Sisterhood Is Global Institute, and cofounder (with Jane Fonda and Gloria Steinem) of the Women's Media Center. She currently writes and hosts *WMC Live with Robin Morgan*, a syndicated weekly radio program with a national and international audience in 110 countries around the world.

Kathy Najimy is an actor, director, writer, producer, and activist known for her memorable performances in more than twenty-five films and one hundred television projects. As a proud feminist and social justice advocate, she has been recognized with numerous honors for her enthusiastic work supporting women's, girls', and LGBTQ rights, AIDS awareness and prevention, animal rights, and reproductive rights. She frequently travels the country as a keynote speaker on these issues.

Ana Navarro is a Republican strategist, CNN political commentator, Telemundo contributor, and cohost of *The View*. She was the national Hispanic campaign chairwoman for John McCain in 2008 and national Hispanic co-chair for Jon Huntsman Jr.'s 2012 campaign.

Gavin Newsom is the governor of California, serving since January 2019. Prior to that, he was lieutenant governor of California from 2011 to 2019 and was mayor of San Francisco from 2001 to

2011. He is the author of *Citizenville* and married to filmmaker Jennifer Siebel Newsom.

Jennifer Siebel Newsom is a filmmaker, CEO, advocate, thought leader, and the founder and chief creative officer of The Representation Project, a nonprofit organization that uses film and media as a catalyst for cultural transformation. Her documentaries *Miss Representation* and *The Mask You Live In* explore the ways gender norms and stereotypes negatively impact girls and boys. Married to the governor of California, Gavin Newsom, she is the First Partner of California.

Christiane Northrup, MD, is a bestselling author, board-certified OB-GYN physician, and a pioneer and leading authority in the field of women's health and wellness, which includes the unity of mind, body, emotions, and spirit. Internationally known for her empowering approach to women's health and wellness, she teaches women how to thrive at every stage of life.

Eleanor Holmes Norton is a Democratic US representative serving the people of the District of Columbia since 1991. Before that, President Jimmy Carter appointed her to serve as the first woman to chair the US Equal Employment Opportunity Commission. She came to Congress as a national figure who had been a civil rights and feminist leader, tenured professor of law, and board member at three Fortune 500 companies.

Soledad O'Brien is an award-winning journalist, documentarian, news anchor, and producer. She is the founder and CEO of Starfish

Media Group, a multiplatform media production and distribution company dedicated to uncovering and investigating empowering stories that look at the often divisive issues of race, class, wealth, poverty, and opportunity through personal narratives.

Sandra Day O'Connor was the first woman justice to serve on the Supreme Court of the United States. She founded iCivics, a website dedicated to providing creative and effective teaching tools on the subject of civic engagement.

Brittany Packnett is an award-winning activist, educator, organizer, and writer who has committed her life and career to justice. She was a Fall 2018 Fellow at Harvard Kennedy School's Institute of Politics; is cofounder of Campaign Zero, a policy platform to end police violence; and cohost of the award-winning podcast *Pod Save the People*. She currently writes a column for *Teen Vogue* called "Listen Up!"

Dolly Parton is a singer-songwriter, author, actress, and philanthropist and is the most honored female country performer of all time, garnering eight Grammy Awards, a Lifetime Achievement Award, and more than a dozen other awards throughout her career spanning more than five decades. She founded the Dollywood Foundation, which funds Dolly Parton's Imagination Library.

Nancy Pelosi made history in 2007 when she was elected as the first woman to serve as Speaker of the House of Representatives. Now in her third term as Speaker, she made history again in January 2019 when she regained her position as second-in-line to the presidency, the first person to do so in more than sixty years. She is the author of *Know Your Power: A Message to America's Daughters*.

Amy Poehler is an Emmy Award– and Golden Globe–winning actress, as well as a writer, producer, director, and author of *Yes Please*. She is active in women's issues and serves as ambassador for the Worldwide Orphans Foundation. Onscreen and off, Amy believes in empowering women and girls everywhere. Through her digital series Smart Girls, Amy continues to acknowledge and support girls who are "changing the world by being themselves."

Ai-jen Poo is a labor activist, organizer, and author. She is the director of the National Domestic Workers Alliance and co-director of the Caring Across Generations campaign. She is a 2014 recipient of the MacArthur "Genius" Award and the author of *The Age of Dignity: Preparing for the Elder Boom in a Changing America*.

Natalie Portman is an Academy Award– and Golden Globe–winning actress who has appeared in more than forty films. In 2004 and 2005, she traveled to Uganda, Guatemala, Ecuador, and Mexico as the Ambassador of Hope for FINCA International, an organization that promotes micro-lending to empower women in poor countries by helping them start their own businesses.

Amy Richards is a writer, producer, and organizer. Most recently, she produced the Emmy-nominated series *Woman* for the Viceland channel and was a consultant on the PBS documentary *Makers: Women Who Make America*. Author of *Opting In* and coauthor of *Manifesta* and *Grassroots*, Amy's writings have appeared in most major publications. She is also the president of Soapbox Inc., the foremost feminist lecture agency, and the affiliated Soapbox Foundation, creators of Feminist Camp. She is the cofounder of the Third Wave Foundation, a national organization for young feminist activists.

Cecile Richards is a nationally respected leader in the field of women's health, reproductive rights, and social change. For more than ten years, Richards served as president of Planned Parenthood Federation of America and the Planned Parenthood Action Fund. She is a frequent speaker and commentator on issues related to women's rights and activism, and is the author of *Make Trouble: Standing Up, Speaking Out, and Finding the Courage to Lead—My Life Story*.

Mary Robinson was the first woman president of Ireland. She is a former UN High Commissioner for Human Rights and chair of The Elders—an independent group of global leaders working together for peace, justice, and human rights. She is an advocate for gender equality, women's participation in peace-building, and human dignity.

Ileana Ros-Lehtinen is a former Republican congresswoman who served Florida's Twenty-Seventh Congressional District from 1989 to 2019. She was the first Latina elected to the US Congress and the first Republican in Congress to publicly support the passage of the marriage equality act. She is currently a Distinguished Presidential Fellow at the University of Miami.

Sheryl Sandberg is the chief operating officer of Facebook and founder of the Sheryl Sandberg & Dave Goldberg Family Foundation, a nonprofit organization that works to build a more equal and resilient world through two key initiatives, LeanIn.org and OptionB.org. She is the author of *Lean In: Women, Work, and the Will to Lead* and coauthor of *Option B: Facing Adversity, Building Resilience, and Finding Joy.*

Stephanie Schriock is the president of EMILY's List, an organization that has helped elect record numbers of women to the House and Senate, and has recruited and trained hundreds of pro-choice Democratic women to run for office. She is also the president of American Women, a research organization affiliated with EMILY's List, which seeks to increase public awareness of the issues impacting women and families.

Debbie Wasserman Schultz is a Democratic US representative serving the people of Florida's Twenty-Third Congressional District since 2005. She is an advocate for women and girls and is the author of *For the Next Generation.*

Maria Shriver is a Peabody Award– and Emmy Award–winning journalist and producer, an NBC News Special Anchor, and founder of The Women's Alzheimer's Movement, Shriver Media, and The Sunday Paper. She is also the author of seven *New York Times* bestselling books, including her most recent title, *I've Been Thinking . . .*

Rachel Simmons is a bestselling author, educator, and consultant who helps girls and women be more authentic, assertive, and resilient. She is currently the director of the Phoebe Reese Lewis Leadership Program at Smith College. She is also the cofounder of the national nonprofit Girls Leadership and the author of *Odd Girl Out*, *The Curse of the Good Girl*, and *Enough As She Is*.

Anna Deavere Smith is an actress, playwright, teacher, and author. Smith costars on the ABC/Shonda Rhimes series *For the People* and appears on the hit ABC series *Black-ish*. Her most recent play and film, *Notes from the Field*, looks at the vulnerability of youth, inequality, the criminal justice system, and contemporary activism. She is the founding director of the Institute on the Arts and Civic Dialogue at New York University, where she is also university professor at NYU Tisch School of the Arts.

Olympia Snowe served as a Republican US senator for Maine from 1995 to 2013 and was known for working across party lines during her time there. Before her election to the Senate, she represented Maine's Second Congressional District in the US House of Representatives for sixteen years.

Gloria Steinem is a renowned writer, speaker, and feminist activist. In 1972 she cofounded *Ms.* magazine, which has become a landmark in both women's rights and American journalism. She also cofounded the Women's Media Center and the National Women's Political Caucus. Her books include the bestsellers *My Life on the Road*, *Revolution from Within*, *Outrageous Acts and Everyday Rebellions*, and *Moving Beyond Words*.

Loung Ung is a survivor of Cambodia's killing fields and is a best-selling author, activist, and co-screenplay writer of a 2017 Netflix original movie directed by Angelina Jolie based on her memoir, *First They Killed My Father.*

Jessica Valenti is a feminist author, Medium columnist, and cofounder and former executive director of the award-winning blog Feministing.com. Her most recent book, *Sex Object: A Memoir*, is a *New York Times* bestseller.

Diane von Furstenberg is a fashion designer, author, and philanthropist best known for designing the iconic wrap dress in 1974. An active philanthropist, she sits on the board of Vital Voices, an organization that empowers emerging women leaders, and also serves as a director of The Diller–von Furstenberg Family Foundation, through which she has donated to several important causes.

Alice Walker is a bestselling author of many volumes of poetry, powerful nonfiction collections, and literary fiction, and she was the first African American woman to win a Pulitzer Prize for fiction with her novel *The Color Purple*, which also won the National Book Award. She is an activist who has worked to address problems of injustice, inequality, and poverty.

Kerry Washington is an activist, producer, and award-winning actor known for starring in ABC's hit TV drama *Scandal*, several movies, and, most recently, in *American Son* on Broadway. She is active in many social and political causes. In 2013, she was honored with the NAACP President's Award, which recognized her special achievements in furthering the cause of civil rights and public service.

Maxine Waters is a Democratic US representative serving the people of California's Forty-Third Congressional District since 1991. She made history as the first woman and first African American chair of the House Financial Services Committee. She has gained a reputation as a fearless and outspoken advocate for women, children, people of color, and the poor.

Jody Williams, a lifelong advocate of freedom and civil rights, received the Nobel Peace Prize in 1997 for her work to ban landmines. She is cofounder and chair of the Nobel Women's Initiative, which amplifies the work of grassroots women's organizations and movements around the world. She holds the Sam and Cele Keeper Endowed Professorship in Peace and Social Justice at the Graduate College of Social Work at the University of Houston, where she has been teaching since 2003. She is the author of *My Name is Jody Williams: A Vermont Girl's Winding Path to the Nobel Peace Prize*, her memoir on life as a grassroots activist.

Marianne Williamson is an internationally acclaimed author, spiritual leader, lecturer, activist, and teacher. Many of her books have been *New York Times* bestsellers, including the popular title *A Return to Love*. Her latest book is *A Politics of Love: A Handbook for a New American Revolution*. She previously ran for office in 2014 as an independent candidate to represent California's Thirty-third Congressional District. In January 2019, she announced that she is running for president in 2020.

Oprah Winfrey is a media mogul, philanthropist, actress, producer, and author. For twenty-five years she was the host and supervising producer of the top-rated, award-winning *The Oprah Winfrey Show*. She also created the Oprah Winfrey Network (OWN), *O, The Oprah Magazine*, and the Oprah Winfrey Leadership Academy for Girls in South Africa.

Julie Zeilinger is the founding editor of WMC FBomb, a feminist media platform on Women's Media Center for teens and young adults. She is the author of *College 101: A Girl's Guide to Freshman Year* and *A Little F'd Up: Why Feminism Is Not a Dirty Word*.

ACKNOWLEDGMENTS

I am incredibly grateful to have interviewed so many truly extraordinary thought leaders, many of whom are featured in this book, who have individually and collectively contributed to so much transformative change in the world. Those interviews and interactions have guided me, and I continue to channel and use the wisdom I have gained. This book is a way of honoring and celebrating all their powerful words of hope, insight, and inspiration so their words can further inspire and propel change.

I am also thankful to all the many colleagues and partners who have mentored, collaborated with, and supported me and my work throughout the years.

I would like to thank Simon & Schuster and Tiller Press, which has been a wonderful and supportive home for this project, and in particular Lauren Hummel, who offered insightful and helpful suggestions, edits, and encouragement along the way, as well as Theresa DiMasi and Anja Schmidt for believing in this book from the beginning and all they did to make it possible.

And I am deeply grateful to my friend and longtime brilliant editor Angela Joshi. She and I met when we worked together on my first book, *Daring to Be Ourselves*, and then I asked her to work with me on my second book, *What Will It Take to Make a Woman President?*, and it has been a blessing to work with her again on this book as well. Because she has worked with me on every book and on so many of my interviews and articles I have written over the years, she knows the catalog of my interviews better than anyone. So when it came to doing this book, and helping to select quotes, organize them into chapters, and edit them down to their most potent distillment, she was invaluable. I simply could not have done this book without her. More than that, she is always so wonderful to work with. I feel incredibly lucky to have her as a partner in all my work.

I also want to send love and thanks to my parents, Norman and Carol Schnall, who have nurtured, encouraged, and cared for me in so many important and vital ways.

I am also forever grateful for my husband and soul mate, Tom Kay, who is such a loving and supportive life partner and an incredible father to our two daughters. And to my remarkable powerhouse daughters, Lotus and Jazmin: I love you beyond words and learn from you both every day. It has been my honor to be your mother and watch you grow into the extraordinary young women that you both are, and I could not be more proud of you.

And to all those who are reading this book: thank you for all you are doing to be a positive force for change. Individually and collectively, we are all leading the way toward a more inclusive, diverse, and equal world.

ABOUT THE AUTHOR

Marianne Schnall is a widely published writer and interviewer whose work has appeared in a variety of media outlets including *O, The Oprah Magazine*, TIME.com, *Forbes*, CNN.com, Refinery29, Women's Media Center, The Huffington Post, and many others. Schnall is the founder of Feminist.com, a leading women's website and nonprofit organization, and WhatWillItTake.com, a media and event platform that engages women everywhere to advance in all levels of leadership and take action. She is the author of *What Will It Take to Make a Woman President?, Daring to Be Ourselves,* and her new book for girls, *Dare to Be You: Inspirational Advice for Girls on Finding Your Voice, Leading Fearlessly, and Making a Difference.*